B1ZOLOGY® 101

YOU + NUMEROLOGY = BUSINESS SUCCESS

B1ZOLOGY®
—— with Jo Soley ——

Dedication

This book is dedicated to Richard Abbot.

A guiding hand and a strong mentor in supporting the birth and growth of Bizology®. For showing me that there are two things going on, what is going on and what is really going on.

CONTENTS

FOREWORD

"You're not the number next to you". I hear this sentence ring through my mind in a soft British accent that commands a rare, quiet authority. It spontaneously comes to me every time I feel lost, swimming in over my head, or just plain old overwhelmed with the hundreds of micro-decisions I have to make in my life and business to keep going and growing. Every time I hear it, a smile crosses my face and I say a silent prayer of gratitude for Jo Soley - the woman who changed my life with numerology and her Bizology® magic over three years ago.

Like everyone meets anyone these days, I first met Jo on the Internet. I had heard of numerology before and it intrigued me. However, it was always presented in a way that was a little too "woo-woo" for my liking. Don't get me wrong, I love the woo. However, my American southern-girl roots demand tangible, real-world results from everything I invest my well-earned money, time, and energy into. So, like any smart (and sneaky) business owner would do, I internet stalked Jo for a few weeks. I could tell right away she was the real deal because I didn't need a PhD in numerology just to understand her. Like all genuine professionals, she had a knack for presenting advanced and complicated concepts in a no-nonsense way that was easy to understand and apply to my business immediately.

Convinced she had the secret sauce so many of my clients and fellow business owners needed, I invited her to come on my podcast to share her wisdom. After talking to her "in person" and finding that she was all she wrote, I trusted my intuition and instantly hired her to coach me and my entire team through the rapid growth we were experiencing at Atmana Academy, my life coach training and certification company. It turned out to be one of the best business decisions I've ever made.

Discovering my numbers with Jo's approach felt one part electrifying and one part terrifying. As I moved through the process, all the problems, issues, and obstacles in my life and business finally began to make sense. It felt like back-to-back Aha moments of, "that's why I'm the way I am", "that's why I feel the way I feel". I feel a bit sheepish in admitting this, because I'm a classically trained psychotherapist with 20 years of experience. I've invested a lot in my own growth and even more in scaling my business but, as I review the tape, it was working with Jo and implementing what she taught me that moved the needle the most.

This was the case for my team too. Not only did each of them feel a stronger sense of connection to their unique talents and purpose in their work, they also grew more committed to my company's vision, mission and goals each day. I became a better CEO (Life Path 8) and leader too, because I understood what made each of them tick at a deeper level. I felt empowered to challenge them to be bolder in expressing their 'ultimate goal' than ever before. The bottom line here is that the tangible and intangible results of using numerology in your business cannot be overstated. I am thoroughly convinced that Atmana Academy became a seven-figure company due to the amazing work Jo and I did together. If you read this book and take action on what you learn, you'll create amazing results like this for yourself too.

It's been three years, and I'm still coaching with Jo to this day. In fact, I have a session scheduled with her this week. In my 20-year career as a professional mental health therapist, intuition teacher, life coach educator, and entrepreneur, I have had many, many mentors. Jo is at the top of that list. It's been years, but with her guidance, I'm still eagerly and happily unravelling the numbers that tell the story of my business and my purpose in this world.

I can attest with total confidence that within the pages of this delightful book, you find all the magic, mystery and practical steps that you need to harness the power of your life's deep purpose. You are not the number next to you. The world needs you to become the person you were born to be, so you can give it the gift that only you can give. This book - Bizology® 101 is your instruction manual and your numbers are the map. Enjoy the journey - it's the most important one you'll ever take!

Heather Alice Shea, M.S., PCC

Founder and CEO of Atmana Academy

PART 1

INTRODUCTION

CHAPTER 1

HOW WILL KNOWING YOUR NUMERIC ENERGIES HELP YOU IN BUSINESS?

Is there really a benefit to you knowing your numbers?

You may already feel that the world of numerology is fascinating, however I'm writing this book to let you into a secret - understanding your numbers is GAME CHANGING.

It's not only been a game changer for me in my business, but for the hundreds of business owners I've worked with by introducing the concept of Bizology® to supercharge their business.

Your numeric energies show how to manage your business, connect with your audience and bring more flow and abundance (including profit) into your business and marketing.

How? Numerology helps you understand yourself on a deeper level, and anything that helps you understand and connect to who you are as a business owner has to be a good thing, right?

Holistic modalities are becoming more acceptable, however there are some people that consider using numerology in business to be a little 'woo-woo'. When I speak on stage, I often start the talk by saying 'Some call me crazy and some call me for advice', from there I deliver mind blowing insights about the subject - they leave converted.

Let's face it, who doesn't love to discover more about themselves? As a business tool, Bizology® is a pretty powerful discipline.

I care that you get it right

Numerology is becoming more and more popular alongside other holistic modalities. As a result of this, the subject is being dumbed down. It is easy to Google 'How do I work out my Life Path number?' and get it wrong.

I can't emphasise more how important it is to work out numeric formulae correctly, one of the reasons is to ensure we don't lose master number energies. For example, someone may say to me that they are a Life Path 11/2. You are either a Life Path 11 or a Life Path 2, you cannot be 2 numbers at the same time. This also applies to Personal Years, there is a correct way to work them out.

It can be catastrophic if you work out a numeric calculation incorrectly. Sounds dramatic? Read on. If you are currently in a Personal Year 9 which is about endings and you 'believe' that you are currently in a Personal Year 1, which is about new beginnings (as you have used an incorrect calculation), you will be starting all things new when you should be releasing and letting go. You will be working against the vibration of the energy of the year and to be honest that is worse than not knowing which Personal Year you are in!

Are you ready to calculate your numeric energies 'top line' and appreciate what they mean for your business success?

Then let's get to work ...

Why I am using Numerology in Business Coaching

I have always been fascinated by numbers from a young age - numbers not maths or times tables. As a very small girl, I would ask my Mum to write down the names of the students in my class at school and would write numbers against their names. It's as though I remembered that numbers were a familiar energy to me.

As the years went by, every time I saw an article about numerology in a magazine, a book or in later years a blog post or a stall at a Mind Body Spirit fair, I would make a beeline for it. I knew I was a Life Path 1, but didn't appreciate the magnitude of the impact that this has had on my life.

I now 'know' that it is my 'Life's Path' to share the modality of Bizology® - 'Using the Powers of Numerology' in my community, circles and networks and, by using it, create wider communities to complement the over 25 years' experience I have in marketing and business development.

Let me tell you about a defining moment

A few years ago, I attended an event that changed my life. It was a wet evening; 8th March 2017 and Richard Abbot of The Hermitage Development Centre was the guest speaker. He had me at Hello. He spoke for a few hours 'top level' about numerology, its impact on the world, on master numbers, on Trump taking residency in the White House, on Brexit and the fall out. He said forget 'International Women's Day' because it is in fact 'International Women's Millennium!' as we are now in the energy of the 2s – the '2000s'. In numeric terms, 2 is all about the Divine Feminine, Intuition, Sacred Knowledge and the Subconscious Mind (more on this later in Chapter 26).

Over the years I have done a lot of 'work' on myself and studied different modalities, some resonating more than others. However, learning who I am through the lens of numerology, meant that life finally made sense. I realised I'm not a Life Path number 28 10 1, I am a Life Path number 19 10 1 (more on this later in Chapter 23), which is a totally different ball game and at the time I was entering my Personal Year 9, which again has its implications.

Over the course of the year, I learnt much more about the subject, however as I was in a Personal Year 9, it wasn't good timing to embark on something 'new', as when I entered my Personal Year 1, it would have the energy of the 'old'. So, in May 2018 when I was in a Personal Year 1, a year for new beginnings, I studied numerology at a London College.

Since 2017 I have been on a deep and fulfilling journey studying, understanding and working with numerology. I have blended business and numerology, created and trademarked Bizology® and carried out hundreds of Bizology® sessions with my clients. Working with business owners who appreciate that there is a force higher than themselves and who are interested in finding out more to help align with their true path, I purposely launched Bizology® when I was in a Personal Year 1, a year to seed, plant the new and take inspired action. By consciously following the energy of the 9-year cycle one reaps the rewards over the years and, more importantly, as I am aware of this, I have the insight to make it happen.

Some people are naturally curious and sign up for a Bizology® session or a package. After the session they know that they are a Life Path number 3 - The Communicator, or a Life Path number 5 - The Adventurer etc. They appreciate what this means for their lives and their business and how to harness the energy of their number to move forward. They then know the vibration of number 3 is about expression or number 5 is about freedom, and leave the session with a recording, a report and a plan of how to move forward.

Some will keep it at this, as they feel that this is all they need. Some will want to move forward and go deeper. As I know how transformational understanding your numeric energies are, my wish is that they continue. Why?

As this is just the beginning

Understanding your numbers is a journey. The more you learn and apply, the more you understand the subtleties of the numbers. The more you understand the subtleties of the numbers the more you can connect to who you are, how you tick and what you came here to do in this lifetime.

Bizology® is not a one and done

The most important numeric calculation to know and work with is the 'Life Path number', this is also known as the 'Destiny number' - as it says on the tin, it's what you are destined to do in your life and business. In Bizology® 75% of what is going on in your life and business is related to your Life Path number. However, this number is just the starting point towards understanding your numeric chart.

There are 7.9 billion (ish) people in the world, so we don't just divide everyone into 11 numbers, that is like saying I am Aries and you are Leo. Astrology goes so much deeper than just a Sun Sign. Appreciating your full numeric chart including the energies of your name and the Personal Year that you are currently in gives you permission to run your business and live your life from the divine place of uniqueness.

The foundation of Numerology is based on the concept of uniqueness

It is a discipline that recognises every person and every situation as unique. This is its real power and value; one size does not fit all.

There are no mistakes - you are here because you chose to be. There is a supreme destiny over your life. You came here to 'do something' in business and you have all the resources and ability to deal with that 'something', and that 'something' can be found in your numbers.

If you have a number, you have it for a reason

Likewise, if you do not have a number, you do not have it for a reason. Your numbers give you big clues of what you are here to do in your business.

Numerology does not give us the answers, but it shows us where to look

Bizology® is about placing you as a business owner and your personal energies at the centre of all your business efforts to increase impact and connection with your audience.

It is important to be aware of what is going on around you, but you also have to be aware of what is going on inside you, your numbers show you how you can show up, stand up and shine in your business.

I called this book Bizology® 101, because this is literally an introduction to Bizology® and its magic. Even though there is a lot of detail and information, this is only the tip of the iceberg of your Bizology® journey.

Welcome to Bizology®

You + Numerology = Business Success

I look forward to connecting you deeper to your numeric energies in a grounded yet powerful way.

Forget a business plan - let me show you a treasure map ☺

Jo x

CHAPTER 2

WHAT NUMEROLOGY IS AND ISN'T - A BRIEF HISTORY

Numerology is based on ancient, esoteric wisdom. It is a well-established discipline, similar to Astrology but instead of looking to the stars it looks to numbers.

Numerology has been used by celebrities and CEO's across the world as a way of harnessing the subtle energies that are all around us.

Where did it come from?

Mathematicians tell us that numbers rule the world, which may sound a bit Beyonce, but they are right, nothing exists in life without numbers. Numerology is also referred to as 'the science of numbers' drawing together numbers and letters.

Throughout history several numeric systems have originated across various civilisations, time periods and locations across the world. The ancient civilisations of Atlantis, Babylon, China, Egypt, India and Greece, (including various biblical references), each used numerical systems to decode messages in their scriptures. The ancient Babylonians created the Chaldean system, however this is not used as much today as its accuracy is questioned. In 800 BC the Greeks modified the 22 symbol Phoenician alphabet to form their own, which served as the basis of the 26 letter roman alphabet which is used today.

The most popular form of Numerology that is used today is commonly referred to as 'modern' or 'western' numerology. This system is based on the work of the Greek Philosopher and Mathematician Pythagoras, over 2500 years ago. Pythagoras, one of the philosophers of Ancient Europe, is cited to be the 'Godfather' of numerology and the man who put numerology on the map. Born around 590 BC, Pythagoras taught his students an exact mathematical precision:

"The principles governing the numbers were understood to be the principles of real existence; the elements of numbers were the elements of realities".

Pythagoras

His pioneering ideas are based on the foundations of Mathematics, Astrology, Astronomy and Physics. He introduced the concept of the metaphysics of numbers, viewing numbers not just as amounts and measures but as vibrational currency.

Numerology as a modality was born - although the word Numerology was not used until the early 20th century. Numerology we use today is based upon the concepts developed by Pythagoras, he said *"nature geometrizes"*, introducing the theory that every number can be reduced down to a single number, its root, and that this number has a cosmic vibration.

Three women who had a significant influence on modern day numerology were Mrs Dow Balliett, Dr Julia Seton and Dr Juno Jordan. Mrs Dow Balliett's teachings were based on the Pythagorean theory, and her work influenced Dr Julia Seton who travelled worldwide teaching numerology. Her daughter Dr Juno Jordan tested numerological theories for over 25 years concluding - 'Numbers do not lie.'

Numerology is as old as time, **BUT** it is as new as the next decision you are going to make in your business.

What is Numerology?

You may have heard phrases like, 'I've got your number' or 'Your days are numbered' and this is because ...

Numbers speak and their language is Numerology

Numbers are magic, energetic, innate, deep, cosmic. They are fundamental of form. Nothing happens in life without numbers, they are intrinsic to everything we do.

Numerology is a method by which we recognise our divinity and connection. It is a key to freedom. A cosmic clock. A route to self-knowledge and understanding.

Maths deals with quantity, for example, 2+2=4. Numerology deals with stories. Let's take the energy of the number 4. 4 is about structure, control, routine and systems. In life we have 4 fingers, 4 directions, 4 seasons, 4 elements, 4 chambers to our heart, 4 parts of our brain, 4 pairs to our DNA, 4 wheels to a car, 4 walls to a house, 4 legs to a chair, 4 major Archangels, 4 suits in the tarot and a pack of cards, etc. 4 literally keeps us on track in life.

Every number tells a story, throughout this book I will be sharing with you the story that your numbers are telling you in business.

Numerology IS ...

- Based on the fact that numbers are energy.
- About sensing the energy of the numbers, using information and then our intuition.
- Used as a route to self-knowledge and self-understanding.

Numerology ISN'T ...

- About accumulating lots of information about a number (and going down rabbit holes).
- A method of defining people in a fixed or limited way OR a way to predict the future, although Personal Years can give us huge clues to what is currently going on in our life

and business.

- Just about using Apps for automated readings, as there is an intuitive element to it.

CHAPTER 3

NUMEROLOGY FOR A BETTER BUSINESS

You may have heard phrases like, 'There is no cookie cutter approach in business', 'There is no magic formula in business' or 'What got YOU there will not get ME there', but it is all true!

You are unique and I am unique. We all have a unique set of numbers in our numeric chart, and our numbers show us who we are and what we are here to do in life and business, in a unique and different way.

Bizology® is a whole new way of doing business

It is primarily about placing you as a business owner and your personal energies at the centre of all your efforts and activities. A conscious way of doing business, driven by what your numbers say.

In these current challenging times, we have to have a deeper understanding of ourselves

Your numbers show you how you can be resilient, how you can thrive in times of stress and how you personally manage stress. Essentially under stress the negatives of your numbers will quickly show, understanding these helps you strengthen your character and resolve.

When it comes to using numerology to help create more success in life and business it's actually very simple. Once you have an understanding of your numeric energies, the most important thing to remember is that we are the negative of our numbers.

Everything else, all other information related to your numbers, including the information you will read in this book, is just guidance. When you stop playing out the negatives of your numbers, when you are consciously aware of the challenges that these bring to your lives, then the positives naturally flow.

Why it is important to understand your numeric energies as a business owner ...

It's pretty mind blowing. I always see people's eyes widen when I connect them to their numeric energies. I witness their 'Aha moment' - 'Light bulb moment' in action. That is the immense power of numerology, its ability to help you understand your depths like nothing else. A client once said to me 'numerology cuts through years of therapy ...' it does.

You are here to do a 'job' in the world. You are here to do a 'job' in your business, and this 'job' can be found in your numbers. Your numbers give you clues relating to what you are here to create, build and grow. The good news is, you have been given all the tools you need to do this.

Going deeper, you are here to do a job I can't do and I am here to do a job you can't do, in a specific, numeric unique way. Understanding and analysing our numbers helps us appreciate what we are here to do in our business and birth into the world, as it delivers mind blowing awareness and provides us with the motivation to take action to get the results that we desire with more ease.

It's not just business coaching and it's not just Numerology

As part of your Business Planning and Sales and Marketing Strategy you need the following elements. You need a clear message. You need to understand your ideal client avatar / target market. You need a package staircase of product and service offerings that solve the problem that your ideal client has. You need to establish your pricing. You need a consistent content strategy. You need a sales funnel that converts paying clients.

Before we look at **any** of these elements, we need to first look at YOU. The business owner, the person that is running your business. You are THE most important asset you have in your business, so it is important that you understand who you are and numerology is the perfect methodology to show you this.

You may have heard the phrase, 'People do business with you if they like, know and trust you', well Bizology® helps you like, know and trust yourself! Most people don't know who they are. I didn't understand myself before I started to study Jo Soley through the lens of numerology.

Numbers are so powerful they speak to you, they walk alongside you, this helps you move forward purposefully in business.

Your Business Your Way

A fish does not know that it swims in water.

In 2005 I worked in Egypt as a Trading Controller for a large Tour Operator and was based in the resort of Sharm El Sheik. Whilst on a trip to the head office in Luxor, I was with my manager in the hotel lobby waiting for the rest of our team to join us. We were only waiting for 5 minutes and in this time, he decided to tell me about a model called 'The Johari Window'.

Devised by American psychologists Joseph Luft and Harry Ingham in 1955, The Johari Window model is used for understanding and training self-awareness, personal development, improving communications, interpersonal relationships, group dynamics, team development and inter-group relationships.

It is a grid that shows you 4 areas ...

1. What is known by the person about themselves and is also known by others – also called **'the arena'**

2. What is unknown by the person about themselves, but which others know – also called **'the blind spot'**

3. What the person knows about themselves that others do not know – also called - **'the hidden area'**

4. What is unknown by the person about themselves and is also unknown by others – also called - **'the unknown area'**

THE JOHARI WINDOW

	KNOWN BY YOU	UNKNOWN BY YOU
KNOWN TO OTHERS	OPEN ——— KNOWN BY BOTH YOU AND OTHERS	BLIND SPOT ——— UNKNOWN TO YOU BUT KNOWN BY OTHERS
UNKNOWN TO OTHERS	HIDDEN ——— KNOWN TO YOU BUT NOT BY OTHERS	UNKNOWN ——— UNKNOWN BY BOTH YOU AND OTHERS

I remember one of my fellow managers was in disbelief that I was shown this important model literally on the back of a fag packet in 5 minutes as it requires time to digest. That aside, the part that I was confused by and I wanted to understand in more depth was number 2. *What is unknown by the person about themselves, but which others know – also called* **'the blind spot!'**

I could not grasp that there were parts of me that others knew about me that I did not know about myself. That there are parts of us that we are unable to see. Since I have embarked on my journey with numerology, I understand more and more that it is hard for **us** to see **ourselves** clearly and objectively.

Numerology helps us do this, as our numbers help us see the parts of us that we are unable to see. A fish does not know that it swims in water.

Like the Johari Window model, numerology and when used in business Bizology®, helps you ...

- Understand yourself on a deeper level by increasing your levels of self-awareness.

- Improve your communication and interpersonal skills.

- Improve and work on your relationships in group and team situations.

Numerology helps us pinpoint and highlight the energies we are working with, enabling us to step outside of ourselves and examine how these energies influence us in a thousand tiny ways every minute of every day.

Before studying myself through the lens of numerology I did not realise that ...

- I **must** be self-employed.

- I can be so hyper-focused that sometimes I miss out on opportunities.

- I can want all the i's dotted and the t's crossed (and life does not work like this).

- I can be too accommodating and helpful to the detriment of myself.

- I failed to put boundaries in place until it was too late.

Now I know this information, my numbers encourage me to step back and assess situations before it is too late. This will be unpacked for you in more depth later.

CHAPTER 4

WHAT IS BIZOLOGY®?

Bizology® is my unique method helping you understand who you are as a business owner so that you can ...

1. REVIVE your enthusiasm for your life and business.

2. RENEW your commitment to your life and business.

3. RECONNECT to your purpose in your life and business.

A '3 in 1' action method – like a power pod!

Bizology® helps you piece together who you are and ...

- Embrace your business from this new knowledge.

- Uncover a new understanding of how to approach your business, to accomplish your goals at your pace.

- Provide you with clarity on your personal business direction, not trying to fit in with paths prescribed by others.

Bizology® opens your eyes to operating your business in a unique way that suits you, shines a light on parts of you that have felt missing and identifies emotions that you can't quite put your finger on. By using this approach you can be visible without feeling vulnerable, master how your unique personality works when marketing your business, and always feel supported by your numeric energies.

There are better years and easier years to do things

We work in 9-year cycles and there are better years to start something new and there are better years to let go and release the old. Understanding this helps you feel less overwhelmed in certain years, focusing and directing your energies by planning for the upcoming months and years. Maximising your business impact by becoming more strategic using the cosmic currents helps you to align to better business decisions.

Looking back at past cycles helps you understand the decisions and directions that you have taken over the years. There are no mistakes - divine timing is a thing. We delve more into cosmic currents and the 9-year cycle in Part 3 of this book - 'Using Cosmic Currents in Business.'

Bizology® helps you channel your strengths

Confidently moving forward in your business with knowledge and insight, from this fulfilled place means that you can choose your business direction enabling your personal business superpowers to shine.

Bizology® helps you optimise your business success, creating a plan from a place of self-appreciation and self-acceptance, working with your strengths and becoming aware of your personal challenges.

Bizology® helps you find the missing piece in your business

Enabling you to build stronger foundations, giving you deep insights into yourself and providing clear ideas to take your business forward. Helping you as a businessperson to achieve success.

- Getting you super clear on your business message.

- Getting you super clear on what you share in your marketing content.

- Getting you super clear on your business direction.

Bizology® is for you if ...

- You are setting up your business.

- You are reshuffling your business.

- You are up levelling in your business.

Bizology® helps you make better business decisions

Bizology® assists you to develop a clear business plan and approach to communicating in your business. Helping you put all the pieces of the business jigsaw together, so that you can play to your strengths and understand why some approaches do not work so well for you.

Providing you with light bulb moments, appreciating that there are greater forces at play. Highlighting your superpowers and identifying the areas for growth. Giving you a clearer vision for future direction by helping you feel re-energised and more motivated to run your business.

Bizology® is revolutionary

Helping you activate your numbers to work at optimum performance. A high-performance tool in your business toolbox aimed to help you achieve goals. The 'business cookie cutter approach' doesn't work, as you have your own unique business imprint and the ways in which to play to these strengths and these qualities are shown in your numbers.

This shows you how to appeal to ideal clients and collaborators by being your true authentic self, giving you permission to be who you truly are in business.

Bizology® provides mind blowing insights

So that you can ...

- Make bold decisions instead of procrastinating in your

business.

- Understand yourself / co-workers / collaborators / team and family (as life is also business) on a deeper level.
- Follow your true business path confidently and with more ease.
- Perform at your peak (at the right time).
- Strengthen your business intuition.
- Identify what is important and what is missing and how and when to move forward.
- Gain clarity and perspective on how you manage your business.
- Move forward in business truly aligned.

Supporting you to ...

- Get clear on your mission, vision and core values.
- Get clear on your ideal working week and what this entails.
- Create products and services that are aligned and stand by your business offerings.
- Understand what you bring to the table - how you help people, by being clear on the benefits you offer.
- Own and articulate your key message so your ideal client will hear you.
- Understand your unique approach to relationship marketing.
- Ensure that your brand is aligned and reflects your numeric positioning.
- Understand what on and offline marketing works for you in line with your numbers.
- Lead from the front in your sales calls, developing trust and rapport with your prospects and handling

objections with ease.

- Make clear invitations to work with you as you understand who you are.
- Stay completely in your business lane intuitively knowing what works and saying NO to everything that is not in alignment with that.
- Discover and work with your numeric energies helping you improve your creativity and productivity, develop better client relationships and increase profitability.

Jo Soley in numbers

I am working with the energy of the Life Path 1 - The Leader. In Part 2 of this book I will show you how to work out your Life Path number and what this means for your business success. Once I embodied this knowledge, everything fell into place.

How has understanding my numeric energies helped me in my business?

Life Path 1 = The Leader = Leadership

Owning this and not following the crowd has opened many doors for me in business.

As I have made my life about me ...

Before I really appreciated this, I definitely made my life all about other people, and put myself last, I was the ultimate people-pleaser. Some Life Path numbers are here for the 'service over success' piece, but not Life Path 1s.

Life Path 1s need to make their life about them and from this place they help other people.

I was great at being a 'number 2', the power behind the throne for other business women. I was constantly working in groups and taking part in joint ventures and business partnerships. My business was not really working for me, as I am **not** meant to be doing these things. I am meant to be a Life Path 1, The Leader, The Discoverer, The Innovator, The Pioneer, The Trail Blazer, The Torch Bearer, The Trend setter. Since I have embraced this energy, my life and in turn my business is working, as I am aligned with who I am meant to be at soul level by using the innate gifts and qualities that I have been given.

It sounds selfish, it's not, it's about self-preservation, putting my head down and getting on with what I am here to do, not worrying about what others are doing and from this place serve others.

I HAVE to be self-employed ...

For over 10 years, I travelled the world, I had the most incredible jobs in the Travel and Tourism Industry in the most amazing countries and stunning locations all over the world. I lived in Austria, Australia, Egypt, France, Greece, Greek Islands, Morocco, Oman, Portugal, Turkey, Tunisia etc. When people ask me where I used to live, I joke that it is easier to ask me where I did not live.

Despite this I was never happy being employed. I dislike restrictions, being told what to do and taking orders from others. Doing my thing, my way is critical for a Life Path 1. At the time of writing this book, I have been self-employed for over 9 years, but it is only the last 5 years since I launched Bizology® that I have really understood what I am here to do in the world.

This helps me consciously take charge of my life and make my own decisions in business. There is a lot of fear in the world and it is fair to say we are in times of crisis, so it is critical I keep on my business path, and understanding my numeric energies helps me do this.

Individuality, Independence, Innovation ...

Being self-employed is not enough. My Life Path 1 is also about all things new - original ideas and innovative concepts. Introducing Bizology® by blending numerology and business coaching is a unique and individual concept that I have birthed into the world, in alignment with my numbers, and it is working for me, my clients and my community.

The New ...

Life Path 1 energy is all about the new, however we are the negatives of our numbers, (a concept I will reiterate during this book), taken to the extreme for a Life Path 1 this can be countries, careers, jobs, houses, relationships etc. Looking back, I can see that my pattern was to rush head-first into new experiences all the time. Hence living in over 15 countries, 40+ houses, and I have a few relationships under my belt!

The tendency for a Life Path 1 is to jump over a mountain and then look behind them. I now ensure that I have this pattern in check, not throw the baby out with the business bathwater, letting things land before I automatically switch them up, so that I can build sustainable success. This alone is a huge realisation in terms of understanding my patterns of self-destruction and something for me to watch out for, as we can revert back to our patterning especially in uncertain times.

Doesn't want advice but needs to learn to listen to others ...

Guilty as charged. I have consciously worked on this as I really dislike being told what to do. Other points of view are valid and it helps for me to listen and integrate them into my life and business. The trick is to have the advice as a side dish, as a Life Path 1 I need to make my decisions, whilst at the same time being open to others opinions.

Riding the tide ...

With Life Path 1 there is a tendency to struggle with taking the rough with the smooth. Coupled with impatient tendencies, this can lead me to having very strong desires to leave situations that are not working for me, rather than stay around to see them through. Awareness is the key to change; I can sense check to ensure this is not happening and that I am not making things harder than they need to be.

The Lone Ranger ... Must acquire and then maintain independence ...

Life Path 1 is about independence, however at times this can manifest as co-dependency, I went there and got the t-shirt. I can 'want' a loving relationship; however, I do not 'need' one and there is a difference. I need to maintain independence in all my relationships as Life Path 1 is about standing on my own two feet and being self-reliant.

Some Life Path numbers need more connection with others, for example, Life Path numbers 3, 6 and 9, there is no judgement here, it is part of the relationship compatibility of the numbers - see Chapter 22.

The potential negatives of Life Path 1 are ...
Wilful, headstrong, impatient, self-absorbed and selfish ...

As a Life Path 1 I need to make my life about me, however balance is needed here as it obviously can't always be about me!

Hold your horses ...

I am working with a very fast energy. This can apply to everything, so care is needed. To eat properly, not quickly grab something conveniently as I am too busy doing everything else. Time is required to fill the car up with fuel, not drive around on the fumes. Communications and content need to be checked over for errors. Care needs to be taken when doing things at high speed as accidents can occur. Time needs to be taken when making important decisions, things are always easier to get into in business than out of. Slowing down enables the magic to happen in the gaps and the correct decision to be taken.

Not good at seeing the bigger picture, only seeing what's in front of me ...

Being too result driven can mean that I don't stop to smell the roses or look at the bigger picture as it is not a natural skill for a Life Path 1.

I have touched on these areas top line and these may seem relatively small points, however, the results I have seen in my business from understanding that these areas can trip me up and making tweaks and adjustments has been incredible, and yes game changing.

I am being who I am here to be, and from this place have transformed my relationship with myself, others and my bank account.

The good news is that life doesn't need to be as difficult as we make it, we have everything we need right in front of us, just when we need it, if we follow the guidance of our Life Path number.

In 2017 I valued the power behind numerology, a light bulb went on and so much made sense about who I am and what I am here to do in the world. On a daily basis I now see how the subtleties of my numeric energies play such a key part in my life.

Since I have embraced my Life Path 1, I ...

- Have literally been given the keys to freedom in my life and business.

- Understand what I am here to do and how to do it in my business.

- Am connected to what I am here to do – in essence, the path of my life and am enlightened to what is possible for me and my business.

Through strengthening your connection with yourself by identifying and recognising your purpose, you can smooth your business path.

Going deeper, I have a lot of 1 energy in my chart.

My Life Path number is 1.

The first initial of my first name, J = the 10th letter of the Alphabet = 1.

Joanna as a word vibrates at a 1.

There is a lot of 1 as a frequency in my full name - A, J and S.

If 1 were a chakra it would be the root chakra, if it were a colour it would be red, if it were an element it would be fire. If fire is not built on strong foundations it can burn out. I can have a habit of doing this, so with this awareness, my emphasis needs to be on balance.

1 is about directness, leadership, innovation, individuality, independence and entrepreneurship. There are spectrums to the energy of the numbers, at one end of the spectrum 1s can be selfish and make their life all about them, at the other end of the spectrum 1s can sometimes be selfless and 'people pleasers'. As I alluded to above, I know I have certainly been like that in the past. Those who know me will resonate with the above, and those who don't can see how this information can be so useful.

I now appreciate that my Life Path number is just that, very much part of my life, my life story and my destiny. This information has been so incredibly useful to me, that I now spend all my time helping others not to be square pegs in round holes.

Numerology grants access to higher-level business solutions

CHAPTER 5

MISTAKES MADE BY BUSINESS OWNERS NOT KNOWING THEIR NUMBERS

There are no two ways about it, numerology is a fascinating discipline and when used in business, AKA Bizology® it is incredibly powerful, as you can align your business mission, vision and purpose to your numeric energy. Creating a business that is unique to you.

There are a few rookie mistakes that I see being made time and time again when people discover numerology.

Let's discuss the 5 biggest mistakes business owners make when using numerology in business. I have highlighted these to support you, so you do not fall into these common traps.

In at number 1 ... The Life Path number is worked out incorrectly ...

This is disastrous.

The most important number we work with in numerology is the Life Path number (more on this in Part 2 of this book), so if the most important number we work with is not correct, then straight out the gate you are off to a false start.

It is then concluded that 'this X Life Path number / title / description' is not you (no it's not as it's wrong!) so then you are not motivated to look any further.

Computerised / app-based calculations are to be treated with care because these can use incorrect calculation methods.

Please ensure that when you work out your Life Path number in

Chapter 8, you also double check by using my free Life Path App here https://josoley.com/LIFE-PATH-APP/

Various resources will share various ways to work out your Life Path number, however the correct way to calculate it is to use whole numbers as otherwise you could miss that you are working with a master number.

Master numbers carry a completely different energy, are vitally important and should not be overlooked. If you are working with a master number it is important that you know about it! (See Chapter 6).

Close behind at number 2 ... Down a Google rabbit hole ...

It is great that you want to find out more about your number, however as with anything online there is good, bad and indifferent. Immediately googling your numbers causes no end of issues due to the differing quality of the information available.

Once you know your Life Path number, you may want to work out other numeric formulae related to your numeric chart without really understanding what these mean and the impact they have. Different numerologists call numeric formulae different things - you may come across the Destiny number, Personality number, Achievement Number, Balance Number, Soul Number, Attitude Number, Stress Number, Challenge Number, Lesson Number etc.

Remember, we want to understand not only what the key numeric energies are but how they play out, how they relate to us, and how you can use the information to make an impact in your businesses.

Someone once asked me to create a chart using Numerology, Astrology, Human Design and The Enneagram. Between you and me, this would be absolutely insane! The more data, the more confusion, the more confusion the more misconception and misunderstanding. The reason I prefer to use numerology as a modality is because there are less points of reference - meaning that we can keep everything relatively simple and relatable.

I have had situations when clients are in a certain Personal Year but because 'Google' can give you a bad steer when your Personal Year starts, they think they are in the wrong year and act accordingly, no wonder they do not get very far. This is more damaging than not knowing what year you are in, or worse still, telling someone else they are the wrong Life Path number or in the wrong Personal Year 🙁

Next at number 3 ... Not really feeling it ...

You may find out for example that you are a Life Path 6 - The Nurturer. Life Path 6 is about relationships and responsibility, some people have told me that this feels burdensome and not very exciting. It may conflict with how they view their life and business, so they decide that they are not going to work with Life Path 6. End of story.

You have been given your numbers for a reason and it is your job to work with them. Believe me (as I know from experience) life flows a lot better when you work *with* your numbers rather than *against* them.

If they were to look a little deeper, they would appreciate that there is a lot more to being a Life Path 6 than just nurturing others. It is about connection, groups, creativity and justice (and much more) but because they have shunned this, they do not get the chance to embrace their Life Path number 6 and discover the empowering way it works in tandem with the other numbers in their chart.

Following at number 4 ... 75% of what is going on in your business is related to your Life Path number however ...

Remember you are made up of a cocktail of numbers. Your Life Path number is the main number to start with, it is the path you are here to walk this lifetime, however, you are much more than this one number. You are an intricate and delicate balance of a handful of numbers. Some numbers are easier to use than others, so we tend to stay operating in these numbers in our business. I will introduce you to one of these numbers in Part 4.

It is important that you understand the balance and subtlety of the numbers and how they work together. Knowing I am a Life Path 1 - The Leader, is akin to knowing that I am an Aries. Astrological charts go a lot deeper as we are complex beings, it is the same with your numeric chart. Once you have embraced your Life Path number, there are other important numbers you need to understand and work with, helping you manage the interchangeable energy of your whole chart.

5 ... Negative of our Numbers

I regularly connect my clients to the shadow and darker side of their numbers because this is where the growth is. Like weeds in a garden, when we pull them up the flowers have more chance of growing. If a Life Path 5 can work on the fact that they have the habit of not finishing anything and are attracted by 'shiny new object syndrome' then they have got more chance of growing their business from a place of strength being mindful of these challenges. Not to say these things will not play out - but awareness is the key to change.

This is more powerful than knowing Life Path 5 is about adventure, change and growth, as it enables the business owner to be aware of the pitfalls that can trip them up.

CHAPTER 6

MASTER NUMBERS UNCOVERED

No number is better than any other number, but some numbers can see more, be more and do more and these are master numbers.

11, 22 and 33 are master numbers. Well, 44, 55, 66, 77, 88, 99 are also master numbers, but only 11 and 22 can be Life Path numbers, which is the main number we use in Bizology® to navigate your uniqueness as a business owner.

Life Path 11 = The Spiritual Teacher.

Life Path 22 = The Architect of Change.

33 can be found as an energy in the name, and in other parts of your numeric chart but not as a Life Path number. Some people do tell me that they are a Life Path 33, but using the calculation that I am going to show you, they are working with the energy of the Life Path 6 = The Nurturer.

If you are working with a Life Path 11 - The Spiritual Teacher or Life Path 22 - The Architect of Change, you are working with master number energy.

I refer to these numbers as master numbers, sometimes repeated numbers are also referred to as Angel numbers.

Master numbers are change makers

Master numbers are like other numbers on steroids. This is HUGE energy and these people should not be underestimated. If you are working with a master number, it is like 5000 volts is running through you.

A lot of people fall at the feet of master numbers, they literally worship them. They use them in their pricing (without realising the energy of the numbers, what they mean and if they are compatible with their own energies and the energies of their products and services), they leap up and down if they see 11.11, they use them as a sales tool and jump on numeric bandwagons.

This is because they do not understand the enormity of the power that master numbers have. They see what they want to see with the numbers and sometimes this ventures into wishful thinking territory. Working with a master number in your life and business is not to be underestimated, they need to be understood, respected and then activated.

Master numbers are on one hand a blessing, and on the other hand a burden. Master numbers come with extra gifts and talents, which come with harder lessons and bigger expectations. People with these Life Path numbers are here on earth to manage this energy and to overcome big obstacles in their life. Conversely, they can sometimes self-sabotage in their life and business.

If you have a master number anywhere in your numeric chart you can totally deal with it (as if you have a number, you have it for a reason) BUT understanding how to manage it is part of your Life's Path, part of your destiny.

Birds of a feather flock together, so those with master Life Path numbers will have an instant understanding of one another on a deeper vibrational level.

Life Path master numbers in business ...

- Have high aspirations.
- Will be determined.
- Are altruistic.

Life Path master numbers do need activating

A lot of Life Path master numbers struggle to embrace and work with their master number energy, feeling as though they are not living up to the expectation of the energy, instead they find themselves working at the root of their number.

Life Path 11 – The Spiritual Teacher, many work in the energy of 2 - as 1+1 = Life Path 2 = The Sensitive.

Life Path 22 – The Architect of Change, many work in the energy of 4 as 2+2= Life Path 4 = The Builder.

The trick is to get past this and activate the energy of the master number, which is not an easy task, but no one said it would be.

If a person is working with master number energy ...

- It is like rocket fuel - it is not a case of confidence; the engine has already been upgraded.

- A superpower is inside of the person - positive and negative, they can be destructive or can make an impact, the choice is theirs.

- Hard numbers to be, they will experience highs and lows in life.

- Capable of doing big things, they have it in them to be able to do these things - but how?

- They sense they have special powers – they are different, not ordinary.

Master number Life Paths can literally do whatever they want, but these people don't normally get 'on it' until their 40s, 50s, 60s, later in their life, as they can be late bloomers.

Master number Life Paths are …

- Very aware people.

- Here to experience the extraordinary in life and business.

- Here to do something different and to change the world, one person at a time.

- Old souls – cosmically plugged into the Universe, they carry a higher vibration, as they have chosen to come back in this lifetime to make a difference in the world.

- Here to do something big in business and have all the inner tools to do this.

- Bestowed with greater potential for impacting the whole of humanity in business.

The person working with master number energy becomes subject to fate; bigger things happen through them, there are higher forces at work directing them on their Life's path.

Richard Abbot said when Simon Cowell was looking for the X factor, he needed to look for Life Path 11s and 22s ☺

Life Path 11 – The Spiritual Teacher

11 is a higher vibration of 2, we do not reduce 11 to 2 (as 11 is a master number), 11 incorporates everything that the energy of 2 represents, 2 is about emotion, partnership, flow and balance. Then we add the steroids piece, the master number energy resulting in 11, which has the ability to uplift and inspire others.

11 is also made up of 2 x 1s, so it can harness the strength of the 1 = innovation and originality within the spirit of the energy of 2.

Life Path 11 is a demanding number to be, a testing number to be. 11s feel things on a deep level, they have acute feelings and extreme energies and they have deep talents and extraordinary insights. They are here to use their intuition and psychic abilities to deliver exceptional performance.

Life Path 22 - The Architect of change

22 is a higher vibration of 4, and we do not reduce 22 to 4 (as 22 is a master number), 22 incorporates everything that 4 represents – 4 is against change, 22 is totally up for change.

22 is also made up of 2x2s, so it can harness the femininity of the 2 energy = deep intuition and aesthetic gifts.

22 is also made up of 2x11s, so it embodies the essence of 11 = deep spiritual and inspirational gifts.

Life Path 22 can change the world one person at a time. They are here to create an empire and leave a legacy. It is a powerful energy, very capable and high achieving. They know how to create change, make things happen and leave their mark.

Activating Master Number energy ...

We all have free will, so it is common that Life Path 11 - The Spiritual Teacher chooses not to work in the energy of 11 and instead stay in the energy of Life Path 2 - The Sensitive. Life Path 22 - The Architect of Change can choose not to work in the energy of 22 and stay in the energy of Life Path 4 - The Builder.

I have worked with many master number clients, and I see their potential to work in the energy of the master number, but it is very rare that these people operate in the capacity of the number all the time. They also have the tendency to destroy what they have built as the energy is so powerful - which they must be mindful of.

In Chapter 34, I connect you with well-known people and their Life Path numbers. Pay attention to those with master numbers

- they need grit and stamina and have made an impact on the world.

You are also working with master number energy in your business if ...

- You are born on the 11th of the month.
- You are born on the 22nd of the month.
- The initial of your first name is K – the 11th letter of the alphabet.
- The initial of your first name is V – the 22nd letter of the alphabet.
- You are in a Personal Year 11 – An intense Spiritual Year.
- You are in a Personal Year 22 – A transformational year (that not everyone experiences).

I will share more about the above later in this book.

33 as an energy

Adam and Eve had 33 sons. Jesus was crucified at age 33. In Islam there are 33 dwellers in heaven. There are 33 Gods in the Vedic Pantheon. There are 33 vertebrae in the human spine. Water boils at 33 degrees on the Newton Scale.

33 is also often described as Christ Consciousness.

As I have explained, you cannot reach 33 as a Life Path number (contrary to belief), but this can be found in your name and other parts of your numeric chart.

33 recognises a deep need for humanitarian service with acute sensitivity, tending to feel disheartened by the problems and imperfections in the world. 33 is an exaggerated form of 6 (as 3+3=6), understanding empathetically the pain life can subject people to. In light of this it can become too self-sacrificing, therefore those with 33 in their deeper numeric chart will need to recognise the importance of strong boundaries and practice

self-care. However, the need to help and heal brings with it great fulfilment and a sense of higher purpose.

Repetitive numbers and their meanings

I tend not to focus too much on repetitive numbers, the way I work with the energy of numbers is, if you are seeing a repeated number then the emphasis of the number is amplified, below is what I mean...

If you are seeing ...	
111	**New Beginnings** Act, start something new, related to the energy of 1.
222	**Harmony, Relationships, Balance** Sensitivity and patience is required related to the energy of 2.
333	**Communication, Creativity** Share your message and have fun related to the energy of 3.
444	**Support, Structure, Routine** Have a plan by implementing systems related to the energy of 4.
555	**Change, Movement, Travel** Mix things up and shift gears related to the energy of 5.
666	**Love, Community, Family** Connect to others through relationships related to the energy of 6.
777	**Seeking, Analysing, Asking** Investigate and learn related to the energy of 7.
888	**Money, Success, Wealth** Goal set in a professional way related to the energy of 8.
999	**Healing, Helping, Service** Show compassion when dealing with others related to the energy of 9.

If you do see Master numbers as double digits ...

11.11

I do take note of 11.11. This is a double master number, 11 is related to Spirit. I see 11.11 as a message or sign from above, akin to seeing a Robin or a feather. When you see this number sequence, stop and be mindful of what you are thinking, doing or saying in that given moment. What is currently going on in your life and business? ... connect the dots.

22.22

Another double master number, 22, related to transformation and change. I see 22.22 as a sign to step up, that you are ready for your next level, that it is time to play a bigger game.

PART 2

YOUR LIFE PATH NUMBER IN BUSINESS

Throughout this book I will be connecting you to your Life Path number and how you can use it to elevate your business success.

CHAPTER 7

WHAT IS THE LIFE PATH NUMBER?

The Life Path number is the single most important number we use in Bizology®.

In business it shows you the direction to take, the main opportunities you will attract, your talents and characteristics. It shows you more about you and how you operate as a business owner than any other number.

Your Life Path number shows you where you will find your success, power and energy in business. It also uncovers the shadow side of your personality, highlighting the nemesis and negatives, so you can work to rectify these.

Your Life Path number is created from all the numbers in your date of birth. You can't change your date of birth, so your Life Path number does not change. You can't physically be reborn in this lifetime, we speak about spiritual rebirth, but you can't change your date of birth, it is impossible.

Your Life Path number is THE number that you are here to work with and make friends with, the path you are here to walk this lifetime. It is also called your Destiny number, and it is literally that - what you are destined to do in your business here on earth. I don't tend to call it the Destiny number, bringing numerology into business is considered woo-woo enough ☺

Unlike some Personality profiles which change as you grow and evolve, your Life Path number does not change, there are key numbers that always stay with you.

It is important to note that your Life Path number is not

necessarily the easiest number to embody. There are other numbers in your chart that are easier to navigate (more on this later - see Chapter 32), however, it is your Life Path number that you are here to manage and master and from this place you embrace the path your business wants you to take.

Your Life Path number relates to how you operate in your life and business

Understanding your Life Path number ...

- Literally gives you a key to freedom.

- Connects you to what you are here to do in your business.

- Uncovers the possibilities for you and your business.

Through strengthening your connection with yourself and identifying and recognising your purpose, you can smooth your business path.

Most people who have previously encountered numerology will know their Life Path number. When your Life Path number is explained to you, it will feel familiar, as you will, on some level, already be aware of this information.

The trick is, are you working with or against your Life Path number?

If against? How is life working out for you? If you are working in the negative of your Life Path number you will know about it, as your life and business will not flow and you will feel stuck.

Here's the thing, running a business is not easy, if it were then everyone would be doing it. When you understand your Life Path number you are given more insight and intel into what you are here to do in your business.

Working with the energy of your Life Path number helps you navigate your own personal SWOT analysis - Strengths, Weaknesses, Opportunities and Threats, helping you connect to your business vision and mission and share your message in the world, serving your tribe in a way that is aligned with your innate gifts and destiny.

In summary - Your Life Path number in business ...

- Is the main number we work with in numerology, equating to 75% of what is going on in your life and business.

- Is created from the numbers in your date of birth, you cannot change your date of birth it is impossible, so this number never changes.

- Is literally that - the path you came to take in business this lifetime.

- Is also called your Destiny number – what you are destined to do in your life and business.

When you align to this number, your business does not need to be as difficult as you make it.

CHAPTER 8

HOW TO CALCULATE THE LIFE PATH NUMBER CORRECTLY

It is paramount that we calculate this number correctly.

I have created a free Life Path App that you can use here …

https://josoley.com/LIFE-PATH-APP/ - the App takes you to a video of me explaining a little about your Life Path number.

You can also work it out manually. To calculate your Life Path number correctly, take your full date of birth. I have used my date of birth 04/04/1973 below as an example.

When calculating the Life Path number, we use the numbers 1-9, and master numbers 11 and 22.

When calculating the Life Path number, if we encounter a number that is not one of these numbers it gets reduced down.

Add the **whole** numbers together

Your Birth Day *e.g.:* **04** ←

$+$

Birth Month *e.g.:* **04**

$+$

Birth Year *e.g.:* **1973**

Which then gives you a 4-digit number

Total $= $ **1981**

These digits are then added individually

$= 1981 = 1+9+8+1 = 19$

(this is reduced down as we only use **1-9**, **11** and **22**)

$19 = 1+9 = 10$

(this is reduced down as we only use **1-9**, **11** and **22**)

$1+0 = 1$ **The Leader**

My Life Path number is 1 – I am working with the energy of the number 1 = The Leader.

Yes, we all have the ability to be leaders at different times in our lives, but it is Life Path 1s - The Leader, that will embody this ability on a daily basis. Each number has dominant traits that distinguish one Life Path from another.

Please take care when calculating your Life Path number

The reason we use whole numbers instead of individual numbers is that we want to make sure we do not miss master numbers.

If your final calculation is an 11 or 22, do not reduce these to 2 or 4 as 11 and 22 are master numbers

A note on 22 = If your final 4 digits end in 2011, 2002, 2020 or 2200 - this is also Life Path number 22. We gently move 0 out of the way leaving the powerful master number, and 11 is a master number so we do not reduce it further.

Many numerology books and an article that I saved from a popular Sunday magazine states that Oprah Winfrey, Bill Gates and Elton John are Life Path 4s - The Builder. When you read about the energy of the number 4 below you will see that these people are in no way, shape or form Life Path 4s - they are Life Path 22s – The Architect of Change, they are here to do a big job in life and need grit and stamina to do this.

This is why it is so important that we do not 'miscalculate' if someone is working with a master number.

People often say to me that they are 11/2s or 22/4s. Using the methodology I use; you can't be 2 numbers at the same time. You are either a Life Path 11 – The Spiritual Teacher or a Life Path 2 – The Sensitive.

The difference between these numbers is immense, and you will have different tools in your business toolbox to embody these Life Path numbers in business.

In Chapter 23, I share 4 tricky numbers with you that are called Karmic Debt numbers, going deeper with what these mean for your numeric chart and what you are here to learn in your life and indeed business this lifetime.

CHAPTER 9

TITLES AND ENERGIES OF THE LIFE PATH NUMBERS

Titles

Life Path 1 - The Leader

Life Path 2 - The Sensitive

Life Path 3 - The Communicator

Life Path 4 - The Builder

Life Path 5 - The Adventurer

Life Path 6 - The Nurturer

Life Path 7 - The Seeker

Life Path 8 - The CEO

Life Path 9 - The Humanitarian

Life Path 11 - The Spiritual Teacher

Life Path 22 - The Architect of Change

The above are the titles that I use at Bizology® HQ to connect with each Life Path number. If the title I have used does not resonate with you, then connecting to the energy of the number can be challenging.

On the next page I have provided you with other titles that may help you to connect to the energy of the Life Path number.

Life Path 1 - The Leader

The Captain / The Discoverer / The Founder / The Governor / The Ground Breaker / The Guru / The Initiator / The Innovator / The Mover and Shaker / The Pace Setter / The Path Finder / The Pioneer / The Torch Bearer / The Trail Blazer.

Life Path 2 - The Sensitive

The Careful One / The Conscious One / The Co-operator / The Diplomat / The Empath / The Intuitive / The Natural Counsellor / The Peacemaker / The Sensible One / The Team Player.

Life Path 3 - The Communicator

The Actor / The Artist / The Connector / The Correspondent / The Creative / The Entertainer / The Expressor / The Flirt / The Informer / The Socialiser / The Speaker / The Writer.

Life Path 4 - The Builder

The Creator / The Constructor / The Establisher / The Hard-Worker / The Manufacturer / The Planner / The Problem Solver / The Producer / The Worker.

Life Path 5 - The Adventurer

The Dare Devil / The Explorer / The Free Spirit / The Globetrotter / The Risk taker / The Thrill Seeker / The Traveller / The Venturer / The Voyager / The Wanderer.

Life Path 6 - The Nurturer

The Advisor / The Caregiver / The Counsellor / The Guardian / The Liaison / The Lover / The Networker / The Parent / The Perfectionist / The Provider / The Teacher.

Life Path 7 - The Seeker

The Academic / The Egghead / The Genius / The Intellectual / The Mastermind / The Philosopher / The Pundit / The Scholar / The Scientist / The Thinker / The Wise One.

Life Path 8 - The CEO

The Big Cheese / The Boss / The Chair / The Chief / The Director / The Executive / The Goal Setter / The Governor / The Head / The Owner / The Striver / The Top Dog.

Life Path 9 - The Humanitarian

The Activist / The Benefactor / The Charitable One / The Healer / The Helper / The Neighbour / The Philanthropist / The Samaritan / The Scout / The Supporter.

Life Path 11 - The Spiritual Teacher

The Cosmic Connector / The Guru / The Mystic / The Sage / The Shaman / The Spiritual Guide / The Swami / The Wise One / The Witch / The Wizard / The Yogi.

Life Path 22 - The Architect of Change

The Change Maker / The Creator / The Developer / The Engineer / The Inventor / The Improver / The Master Builder / The Originator / The Shape Shifter / The Transformer.

In essence saying the same thing in a different way.

The energies of the numbers are:

1 - The Leader

In the positive ...

Active / Ambitious / Assertive / Authentic / Capable / Competitive / Courageous / Daring / Determined / Driven / Dynamic / Independent / Individual / Innovative / Inventive / Original / Proactive / Self-motivated / Self-starter / Self-sufficient / Unique / Wilful.

Being aware of the negatives ...

Aggressive / Controlling / Defiant / Dominant / Egotistical / Impatient / Impulsive / Insecure / Intolerant / Lonely / Moody / Over-competitive / Selfish / Selfish / Stubborn / Weak-willed.

2 - The Sensitive

In the positive ...

Analytical / Balanced / Considerate / Co-operative / Detailed / Diplomatic / Emotional / Empathic / Gentle / Harmonious / Intuitive / Kind / a Mediator / Patient / Peacemaker / Perceptive / Sincere / Supportive / Tactful / Team-Player / Understanding.

Being aware of the negatives ...

Apathetic / Cowardly / Easily upset / Evasive / Fearful / Fussy / Hypersensitive / Indecisive / Insecure / Jealous / Lacking self-confidence / Manipulative Moody / Over-emotional / Pessimistic / Reticent / Sly / Unpredictable / Worrier.

3 - The Communicator

In the positive ...

Artistic flair / Carefree / Charming / Cheerful / Creative / Energetic / Entertaining / Enthusiastic / Friendly / Fun / Good-humoured / Happy / Imaginative / Intelligent / Joyful / Lucky / Optimistic / Self-expressive / Sociable / Talkative / Warm-hearted.

Being aware of the negatives ...

Attention-seeking / Complacent / Complaining / Critical / Disorganised / Dramatic / Easily bored / Extravagant / Gossips / Inconsistent / Indecisive / Indulgent / Irresponsible / Melodramatic / Oversharing / Sarcastic / Too proud / Vain.

4 - The Builder

In the positive ...

Achiever / Careful / Conscientious / Consistent / Dedicated / Determined / Disciplined / Efficient / Focused / Hands on / Hard Working / Honest / Logical / Loyal / Methodical / Organised / Persevering / Persistent / Practical / Pragmatic / Steady / Systematic / Trustworthy / Worker.

Being aware of the negatives ...

All work and no play / Boring / Controlling / Fault-finding / Inflexible / Intolerant / Narrow-minded / Obstinate / Officious / Perfectionist / Pessimistic / Resisting / Rigid / Stubborn / Too serious / Tunnel Vision.

5 - The Adventurer

In the positive ...

Active / Adaptable / Change-makers / Curious / Energetic / Freedom-loving / Magnetic personality / Mover and Shaker / Multi-talented / Persuasive / Popular / Progressive / Quick learner / Resourceful / Sensual / Talented / Versatile.

Being aware of the negatives ...

Addictive / Easily bored / Impatient / Impulsive / Inconsistent / Indulgent / Intolerant / Irresponsible / Procrastinating / Restless / Scattered / Self-indulgent / Sensationalism / Thoughtless / Unfocused / Unreliable.

6 - The Nurturer

In the positive ...

Artistic / Caring / Compassionate / Conscientious / Creative / Dutiful / Empathic / Forgiving / Good listeners / Harmonious / Helpful / Loving / Loyal / Reliable / Responsible / Serving / Social Consciousness / Supportive / Sympathetic / Understanding.

Being aware of the negatives ...

Bossy / Co-dependent / Interfering / Jealous / a Martyr / Obstinate / Outspoken / Perfectionist / Proud / Resentful / Self-absorbed / Self-righteous / Self-sacrificing / Unsympathetic.

7 - The Seeker

In the positive ...

Analytical / Contemplative / Deep / Inquisitive / Intellectual / Introspective / Intuitive / Investigative / Knowledgeable / Mysterious / Mystical / Observant / Perspective / Reflective / Researcher / Shrewd / Specialist / Wise.

Being aware of the negatives ...

Aloof / Cold / Critical / Cynical / Demanding / Defensive / Distant / Guarded / Highly strung / Impractical / Intolerant / Melancholy / Mental stress / Nervous / Obsessive / Pessimistic / Sarcastic / Sceptical / Secretive / Suspicious / Too serious / Unreasonable / Withdrawn.

8 - The CEO

In the positive ...

Abundant / Achiever / Ambitious / Authoritative / Confident / Courageous / Decisive / Determined / Driven / Executive ability / Goal setting / Good judgement / Integrity / Perceptive / Property / Self-empowerment / Self-motivated / Strong / Successful / Talented in business / Wealthy.

Being aware of the negatives ...

Aggressive / Controlling / Dictatorial / Dishonest / Domineering / Extravagant / Greedy / Hypercritical / Intimidating / Intolerant / Love of power / Manipulative / Materialistic / Mercenary / Ostentatious / Overambitious / Poverty-consciousness / Proud / Ruthless / Superficial / Unscrupulous.

9 - The Humanitarian

In the positive ...

Accepting / Big thinker / Broad-minded / Charismatic / Compassionate / Creative / Diverse / Emotional / Forgiving / Generous / Idealistic / Kind / Healer / Helpful / Open-minded / Passionate / Philanthropic / Reflective / Sensitive / Service / Strong-minded / Sympathetic / The ability to let go / Tolerant / Unconditional love / Understanding.

Being aware of the negatives ...

Daydreamers / Defensive / Faithlessness / Impulsive / Too detached / Indiscretion / Jealous / Melodramatic / Morose / No boundaries / Over-emotional / Over dramatic / Revengeful / Sad / Self-indulgent / Unforgiving / Victim.

11 - The Spiritual Teacher

In the positive ...

Deep / Enlightened / Gifted Healer / Honest / Illuminating / Insightful / Inspirational / Instinctive / having Integrity / Justice / Motivational / Perceptive / Philosophical / Psychic / Refined / Spiritual / Trend spotter / Visionary.

Being aware of the negatives ...

Aimless / Angry / Challenging in energy / Deluded / Demanding / Eccentric / Erratic / Extreme emotions / Fanatical / Highly strung / Hyper-sensitive / Intense / Intolerant / Lack of direction / Nervous energy / Self-denial / Self-destructive / Unstable / Very Introverted.

22 - The Architect of Change

In the positive ...

Accomplished / Ambitious / Creators / Dedicated / Determined / Focused / Forward thinking / Grand scale abilities / Insightful / Inventive / Limitless ability / Limitless potential / Motivated / Powerful / Turn dreams into reality / Visionaries / World is your Oyster.

Being aware of the negatives ...

Controlling / Dark energy / Destructive / Disruptive / Dogmatic / Domineering / Egotistical / Fault finding / Fear of Failure / Fight themselves / Highly strung / Inferiority complex / Inflexible / Overbearing / Perfectionists / Self-sabotage / Stubborn / Talks the talk but does not walk the walk / Workaholic / Wants more more more.

CHAPTER 10

LIFE PATH NUMBER IN BUSINESS - THE BASICS

Some Life Path numbers lend themselves more to running a business than others. Life Path 1 - The Leaders are born to be entrepreneurs. Life Path 5 - The Adventurers are great at conducting global business. Life Path 8 - The CEO intuitively knows what to do in business (and they nail it) and Life Path 22s - The Architect of Change are here to create large scale businesses that transform the world one person at a time.

Every Life Path number can run and/or be part of a successful enterprise. It is about being aware of, tuning into and then harnessing your specific numeric qualities when it comes to running a business.

Life Path 1 = The Leader

One of life's achievers. 1 is about innovation, individuality and entrepreneurship. Bringing fresh approaches into business.

As a Life Path 1 you are born to run your own business and really struggle being employed.

As a Life Path 1 you need to make your life and business about you, and from that place help others.

In business 1s need to positively and constantly innovate and do new things in an original way.

Determined with a courageous and daring streak, this number does not like inaction - it has to be busy.

Your nemesis can be that you can be focused on speed and impatient when creating results.

Life Path 2 = The Sensitive

2 is about flow, harmony, balance and intuition. 2 is connected to divine feminine energy and sacred knowledge.

With the vibration of Life Path 2, quiet persuasion is required instead of force. Life Path 2s are good at seeing both sides of a situation.

In business you work well in groups and teams as it is about cooperation. You work patiently and intuitively with natural knowing.

Worrying about your business can be your nemesis.

** You may have thought you are a Life Path 11 - you can use my Life Path app to double check here -
https://josoley.com/LIFE-PATH-APP/

Life Path 3 = The Communicator

Life Path 3 is about creativity, communication, enthusiasm, optimism and self-expression.

Natural born communicators, 3s are people persons who have the gift of the gab - I mean the gift of divine self-expression ☺

As a 3 you are here to put your word into the world. You are here to achieve success through development of your creative talents.

In business Life Path 3s lead from the front, giving workshops and talks, as you have a talent with words. 3s are the numbers with books in them.

The nemesis for a 3 is that you can take too seriously what others think of you.

Life Path 4 = The Builder

4 is all about structure, control, rules, routine and order.

Life Path 4s are very practical and good organisers; you pay attention to detail.

4s are very hands on and love a strategy, a plan and systems.

4s can be gate-keepers with a rigid approach, so saying no can be your nemesis!

** – You may have thought you were a Life Path 22 – you can use my Life Path app to double check here -

https://josoley.com/LIFE-PATH-APP/

Life Path 5 = The Adventurer

5 is about adventure, change, freedom, growth and expansion.

As a Life Path 5 you can do anything that you are interested in. However, you cannot go through the motions if your heart's not in it. Yes, 5s can do anything, but what should you do?

In business 5 is about all things NEW – new places, new faces and new spaces. As a 5 you love change and can also change your mind a lot!

Freedom is key for a 5, your life truly is about the journey, not the destination.

The trick for 5 is not to become too scattered in the process – that can be your nemesis.

Life Path 6 = The Nurturer

6 is THE relationship and responsibility number and all about love, togetherness, and connection.

6 is the family number, the number of politics, teams, public service, doctors and nurses, teachers and carers.

In business Life Path 6s are deeply invested in connection, you need to feel at the heart of something, be it the business community or the family business.

As a Life Path 6 you are here to give help, service and support when needed.

During this process it is important that as a 6 you do not lose sense of self, this can be your nemesis.

Life Path 7 = The Seeker

7 is about thinking, questioning, seeking, analysing, asking and learning.

7 is the number of the mind – half mysticism and half science.

The goal for a Life Path 7 in business is to use knowledge and wisdom to guide others.

Life Path 7s are the odd ones out, you don't fit in, and you are not meant to.

In business 7s need alone time, time to switch off the noise of the world to retreat and withdraw.

The trick with 7 is not to overthink and procrastinate as this can be your nemesis.

Life Path 8 = The CEO

8 is about success, wealth, property, business, commerce and economics.

8 is considered lucky in many countries – in China and Hong Kong they will pay more to have 8s in the door number, phone number or car registration plate, or will plan special events around the 8th of the month.

8 is THE money number, about making friends with the energy of money, as money gives you freedom of choice.

Life Path 8s nail it in business as you intuitively know what to do. You are here to lead by example, by being professional and having high standards.

The nemesis of 8 is being hyper-critical of self.

Life Path 9 = The Humanitarian

9 is about philanthropy, love, compassion and kindness.

What do we do in the UK when we need help? We call '999' - this is the essence of 9.

As a Life Path 9 you are an old soul; you have been here before. You intuitively know stuff!

In business the essence of a Life Path 9 is 'service over success' and from that place you create prosperity.

The nemesis of 9 is boundaries, the last thing a 9 should do is give up on people but you need to make sure you put your oxygen mask on too!

Life Path 11 = The Spiritual Teacher

11 is cosmically connected and about all things Spiritual – God, Magic, Space, Theorems and The Cosmos.

11 is a master number, and master numbers are supercharged. Life Path 11 is about thoughts and ideas and you are here to be inspired and to inspire others. 11 has the energy of the sensitive and emotional Life Path 2 but on steroids with added edge and energy.

In business as a Life Path 11 you will need to have a direction and a plan.

The nemesis for a Life Path 11 is that you can overreact and be extreme when caught up in negativity, so the need for grounding is important.

** – You may have thought you were a Life Path 2 – you can use my Life Path app to double check here -
https://josoley.com/LIFE-PATH-APP/

(11 energy is quite rare if you were born in the 1900s - there are more being born now in the 2000s).

Life Path 22 = The Architect of Change

Being a Life Path 22 is about changing the world one person at a time in a powerful and successful way.

22 is a master number, you can see more, do more and be more. 11 is about the inner world. 22 is about the outer world.

You are here to create massive change and transform the visible world.

In business you are capable of so much with huge potential. As a Life Path 22 you are here to make things happen; you are here to build megastructures with huge energy.

The nemesis of 22, and therefore the trick is not to work in 4 - which often happens with a Life Path 22 (as 2+2= 4) as your mindset is everything.

** - You may have thought you were a Life Path 4 - you can use my Life Path app to double check here - https://josoley.com/LIFE-PATH-APP/

CHAPTER 11

LIFE PATH NUMBER IN BUSINESS - KEY LESSONS

As a modality numerology helps us decode who we are and what we are here to do on earth, this lifetime.

Running a business is not easy but we can make it more difficult, however by aligning our numeric energies we can find a flow in our business. You do not need to push a cart up a hill or put square pegs in round holes. When you appreciate what numeric energies you are working with, you can align to who you are and what you are here to do in your life and business.

The word healing is used so much in the coaching space and the online world, it is actually a case of learning - through learning you heal. Every day is an opportunity to learn and every day has the potential to teach us something. Life unfolds day by day - what you need in the future becomes available to you when you need it.

You are here to learn in life, and you can see what you are here to learn in the key lessons related to your numbers.

Life Path 1 - The Leader

If you are working with the energy of Life Path 1 you are a born leader and entrepreneur, and you are here to learn ...

Independence – You will learn how to stand on your own two feet in business. Self-employment was made for you; you may avoid it for a while as big life lessons will be found here - we automatically shun what will help us grow the most.

Innovation - Once you are self-employed you need to bring something into the world that is different and only you can do. Going deeper with the concept of uniqueness.

Creation - It is the birth right of the Life Path 1 to bring bold and genius ideas into reality, but this progression needs space not always speed.

Remember you are a pioneer and here to use this progressive energy. Be mindful not to waste time hiding your light under a bushel.

Life Path 2 - The Sensitive

If you are working with the energy of the Life Path 2 ... you are a sensitive team player and you are here to learn ...

Co-operation - You may be (at times) the power behind the throne in business, and that is OK.

Diplomacy - You will always be able to see both sides of the story, so your ability to be impartial serves you well.

Inner knowing - Developing your intuition and managing your emotions – using these skills in a balanced manner in business.

Remember to eat the business elephant with a teaspoon and will need to feel supported by your environment (including team, clients and community) at all times in order to move forward.

Life Path 3 - The Communicator

If you are working with the energy of the Life Path 3 ... you are born a creative expressive and you are here to learn ...

That communication is really your jam – and you are naturally positive and have the ability to express yourself clearly.

If your work brings you joy – it will enthuse and encourage others.

You are here to work - smart not hard.

Remember you are a creative powerhouse who is here to shine bright, however - the brighter the light the darker the shadow, you will find those who are critical of your endeavours, and this can bother you, remember you can't keep all of the people happy all of the time.

Life Path 4 - The Builder

If you are working with the energy of the Life Path 4 ... you are a born organiser and administrator, you are here to learn how to ...

Implement solid plans in business through careful application.

Follow the steady and sustainable path you are The Builder after all.

Be able to change course when needed.

Remember risky start-ups are not for you, slow and steady wins the race, being careful not to be too rigid or inflexible.

Life Path 5 - The Adventurer

If you are working with the energy of the Life Path 5 ... you are a born sassy adventurer, you are here to learn ...

Constant development and growth – but be mindful of always chasing the new, new, new without grounding anything of worth. A tricky balance, remember the rolling stone gathers no moss.

To keep business fresh and exciting - international travel will feature here.

That you must maintain **a sense of freedom** with everything you do.

Remember a 5 can take time to find THE thing they really want to do!

Life Path 6 - The Nurturer

If you are working with the energy of the Life Path 6 ... you are a born nurturer and tribe builder, you are here to learn **...**

That unconditional love is a key ingredient in your business, and a home-based and/or family business will have great appeal.

A one-to-many business model will work well for you - community is your name and relationships are your game.

To let other people make their own mistakes in business and take their own fair share of responsibility, you do not have to do it all.

If you do try to do it all, in time you will resent your clients, community and business - so keep a check on this.

Life Path 7 - The Seeker

If you are working with the energy of the Life Path 7 ... you are a born thinker and seeker, you are here to learn ...

That you are a font of knowledge - this will involve mysticism and science.

That you operate from a different wavelength - and you are meant to - you will not always feel you fit in, and that's OK.

To let others in - especially in business, as you can be fiercely secretive and private.

You will need space from the online world - today's world is pretty busy and crazy, especially for a Life Path 7.

Life Path 8 - The CEO

If you are working with the energy of the Life Path 8 ... you are a born CEO – The Boss, you are here to learn ...

Personal empowerment - helping people raise their business game.

To develop your integrity and never compromise this.

To step into and own your power in business and remember to play a bigger game than the one you are currently playing!

You have the ability to earn and earn well - but it will not be handed to you.

Life Path 9 - The Humanitarian

If you are working with the energy of the Life Path 9 ... you are a born humanitarian with creative flair, you are here to learn ...

What it means to give and receive on all levels. Anything you do in your business needs to come from the place of a passion to help, serve and support.

To implement strong boundaries - as these are vital when you are in the business of giving.

At the same time, never give up on people by learning the power of service over success.

Recognising that some people will not and can not help themselves - be discerning with regards to identifying these people.

Life Path 11 - The Spiritual Teacher

If you are working with the energy of the Life Path 11 ... you are a Cosmic Connector and Spiritual Teacher, you are here to learn ...

That you have powerful abilities accumulating in a higher spiritual calling.

To hone your abilities to inspire others, but you will need to be inspired first.

Not to overreact - working with a master number this energy will feel intense and needs managing.

Ensuring that you balance heart-centred business with an increased level of drive and ambition as you face daily tests along the way.

Life Path 22 - The Architect of Change

If you are working with the energy of the Life Path 22 ... you are The Architect of Change, you are here to learn ...

To create and manage your own enterprise - by putting your name to something in the business world.

Not to get stuck in the details (2+2=4 and 4 = The Builder) and create something of worth to benefit others.

To get out of your own way - mindset is everything.

Remember what you do needs to create an impact and have lasting change for others, not fly by night energy.

CHAPTER 12

LIFE PATH NUMBER IN BUSINESS - YOUR BUSINESS STRATEGY UNLOCKED

> Strategy definition: - *'The word 'strategy' is derived from the Greek word 'stratçgos'; stratus (meaning army) and 'ago' (meaning leading/moving). Strategy is an action that business owners take to attain one or more of their business goals.'*

The key points to remember when you are mapping out your business strategy is -

Be Marmite - Being so right for some people you are so wrong for others. The right people will resonate with your message if it's clear enough.

You Do Need an Ideal Client - A lot of people fear of niching so ...

Get Big, Get Niche or Get Out! - See above ...

One. One. One. One - Focus on ONE product, ONE route to market, ONE avatar and ONE platform – at ONCE.

Get a Message - If you speak to everyone you speak to no-one. Carve your message so your ideal client hears you.

Solve Their Problem - People do not buy their way into something they buy their way out of something. It may feel an old paradigm, but who doesn't want their problems solved?

You Are The Brand - *"Your brand is what people say about you when you are not in the room"* - Jeff Bezos. Invest in it, believe in it and become it, in line with your numeric energies.

The Fortune Is In The Follow Up! - 85% of sales made are between the 5th and 8th point of 1-2-1 contact with someone. When you run your own business, you are also the sales force. Marketing alone is not enough; a sales pipeline is vital too.

Facts Tell Stories Sell - Sales doesn't have to be sticky; it's literally having a conversation with someone about how you can help. The best marketing doesn't feel like marketing, it is about building relationships.

As I have mentioned previously, there is no cookie cutter approach in business and what works for some numeric energies will not work for others.

Some Life Path numbers are very entrepreneurial = Life Path 1, some numbers are executive in energy = Life Path 8, some Life Path numbers are very creative = Life Path 9, below I have given you some insight into what your business strategy should look like based on your Life Path number.

Life Path 1 - The Leader - Business Strategy

- To not actually have a strategy! Sounds crazy, how can you run a business without a strategy? Bear with me, as a Life Path 1 you are excellent at the next thing on your to-do list and then the next thing and the next thing, but if I ask you what you want to do in 5 years' time (even 5 weeks' time) your mind will literally go blank. Here's the thing - you are not meant to know; you are meant to follow the business breadcrumbs.

- 1 is about innovation, leadership and trail blazing – and you can't plan this to the 'nth degree. You need to jump from the steps that show themselves to you from your pioneering discoveries.

- The business strategy for a Life Path 1 needs to be related to forging ahead relentlessly. Life Path 1s are always the first out of the gate so you do well when launching as 1 is all about action.

- You are a whirlwind of thought and activity, however you can lose excitement with ideas, so need a team to support as you come up against roadblocks and detours as you achieve your never-done-before projects.

- When creating your business strategy be careful not to be hyper focused – look up a bit.

Life Path 2 - The Sensitive - Business strategy

- Business partnerships work very well for a Life Path 2 and you do much better in business when you are engaging with others, as you will lead with your heart.

- As a Life Path 2 maintaining a sense of balance in everything you do in your business will be imperative.

- You are sensitive and feel things very deeply, you will really need to love what you are doing in your business, so if your strategy involves your passion, you are off to a good start.

- You don't miss much and are good at attending to the details. You have the patience to create detailed strategy for your business projects in order for the mechanics to run smoothly.

- Create the space to listen to what your market wants and give them the opportunity to ask questions. Take the time to think things through and see things from both sides of the business coin.

Life Path 3 - The Communicator - Business strategy

- Write a book – it's your hook! You may have heard the phrase – add the letters ITY to the word AUTHOR and you are an AUTHORITY in your field - because …

- A book gives you an expert badge, but even more so for a Life Path 3, as you are born authors.

- Find your passion and turn it into your purpose. Cliché? Not for a Life Path 3 - make sure your plans are enthusiastic and optimistic.

- There is an abundance of imaginative energy available to you. Working on anything inspiring and uplifting? Ensure to include this in your concrete business plans.

- Make sure you don't doubt your potential and be careful not to scatter your energy in the process, staying focused is important.

Life Path 4 - The Builder - Business strategy

- Have a watertight plan with strong funnels and systems.

- Pay attention to all the details involved as Life Path 4 thrives where there are established rules.

- Implement these rules and regulations and build upon them to help your business steadily grow.

- Carry out all the details, crossing the i's and dotting the t's of your business strategy.

- For Life Path 4s, strategy is about getting the job done on time and under budget.

Life Path 5 - The Adventurer - Business strategy

- Create revolution in business - mix things up and deliver something unexpected which is out of the blue.

- Freedom is a basic requirement for a Life Path 5, do not tie yourself down in business, have the space to pursue your interests.

- Life Path 5s manifests more business opportunities than any other Life Path number and invariably these will involve global ventures, as 5 is about travel and adventure.

- The issue is keeping tabs on all the exciting developments as the operative word is 'change.' In order to create a strategic plan, Life Path 5s will need flexibility when it comes to the structure of a strategy.

- The business strategy needs to be loose enough to allow flexibility when achieving the end result as the plan may change a few times along the way.

Life Path 6 - The Nurturer - Business strategy

- The business strategy for a Life Path 6 needs to involve the needs of those in your community, so ensure to involve the 2 R's – relationships and responsibility.

- Benefit and help others by building a collective tribal energy. Set up a strong affiliate program using your trusted connections to help you spread your message and magic.

- Life Path 6s needs to be at the heart of something, so your approach will be collective - 'one to many' rather than 121, through programs, courses and groups.

- Align your values to those of your suppliers, clients and

partners as business relationships need to be more than purely transactional.

- Being mindful not to take on too much responsibility and then fail to deliver by taking shortcuts.

Life Path 7 - The Seeker - Business strategy

- Your strategy needs to involve learning, research and development. There are 2 interesting sides to a Life Path 7 – data driven and intensely intuitive.

- Whenever you are learning this is where the growth of the business will come from – the font of knowledge. Literally the more you learn, the more you earn.

- Specialise, be the expert in your chosen field.

- 7 is also about getting the technicalities of the product right – what goes on under the business bonnet, the nuts and bolts, behind the scenes, making sure no stone is unturned when creating and delivering the strategy.

- Be careful not to overthink and under deliver – perfection keeps you poor!

Life Path 8 - The CEO - Business strategy

- Goal setting is important for a Life Path 8, so you will need to factor in business plans, yearly and quarterly plans, marketing and communication strategies more than any other Life Path number.

- All elements of the business strategy should be connected to positioning you as the professional, The CEO.

- 8 is high end, meaning high quality and superior craftsmanship will feature throughout your products and services. Anything high ticket works very well with 8 energy,

VIP days, Immersion Programs, 121 Intensives and retreats.

- Ensure to project manage everything to an executive level, branding, sales copy, emails, graphics – everything should look professional and be on point.

- Be careful not to be hyper critical of self (or others!) if things do not go according to plan.

Life Path 9 - The Humanitarian - Business strategy

- Make your business about other people, Life Path 9s create success when your business strategy is focused on the impact you make in the world. Impact over income.

- As a Life Path 9, you are good at the 'business vision' and just trust it will happen. However, you need support with the details, so make sure you have a clear actionable plan.

- The 'Corporate Social Responsibility' piece is very important as you are here to give back to society in some way.

- This may manifest in the form of setting up a foundation to help those in your chosen field or gifting a scholarship place on one of your programs or membership.

- Be careful not to undercharge and overdeliver, watch those boundaries and serve from the overflow of the cup and not the cup itself.

As we get onto the master numbers, we start to intensify the business purpose.

Life Path 11 - The Spiritual Teacher - Business strategy

- As a Life Path 11, before inspiring other people you need to inspire yourself.

- The business strategy needs to come from above, a force higher than you, driving you towards your inspiration to create your vision.

- Then, when you have a vision, you need a plan.

- 11 is related to all things Spirit but it is also an intense energy and in light of this, Life Path 11s needs a direction to keep them on track.

- 11s can overreact so having a clear path forward helps to minimise this.

Life Path 22 - The Architect of Change - Business strategy

- For a Life Path 22 to work in the energy of the 22 (many work in the energy of 4), it is about discovering a part of you that you did not know exists.

- You need to challenge yourself (and the status quo) to go bigger and then higher, moving past mindset monkeys then to ...

- Create an empire. Leave a legacy. Put your name to something.

- Life Path 22s are looking for the systems that allow the creation of a business, product or service that is not a one hit wonder. If you think you have thought big, it is then about thinking bigger!

- The idea behind your business strategy will be to help people see things they haven't before. Go big or go home with your claims and make sure you deliver, as you know you can.

CHAPTER 13

LIFE PATH NUMBER IN BUSINESS - CREATING YOUR BUSINESS MESSAGE

Are you charging too little? Do you have to work crazily hard to make any money? Are you exhausted as you scrabble to find more and more clients? Do you get frustrated as you know you can help people but struggling to put this in words to convert clients?

The main reason you are not making the money you say you want is that your message is not clear as people do not know what you do.

In simple terms people want their problems solved. In a busy online crowded marketplace, it is not who shouts the loudest, it is who is the clearest with their message.

However, Bizology® is about **YOUR** message in line with your numeric energies. There are clues about what you are here to do in the world related to your numbers =
THE REAL MAGIC IN YOUR MESSAGE.

But first the technicalities ...

WHY do you need a message?

HOW do you carve your message?

WHY are you fearing to niche?

AND then the Magic Sprinkles – YOUR NUMERIC ENERGIES.

After I have shown my clients their numbers through the lens of Bizology® – I work with many of them with their marketing.

I have a 7 Step Process which Covers:

1. **CONNECTION** – How to carve your message so it carries impact, and your ideal client hears you.

2. How to identify your ideal **CLIENTS** and how this assists in the marketing process (commonalities not exclusion).

3. How to get total **CLARITY** on the biggest problems your ideal clients face and the solutions you provide.

4. How to **CREATE** a package staircase of products and services to get your clients results and reinvesting in you.

5. How to create **CONSISTENCY** in your marketing and branding.

6. How to ensure the **CONTENT** you are sharing with the world adds value, is consistent and persistent and carries strong calls to action.

7. How to **CONVERT** all of this into a steady flow of ideal clients to achieve the financial results that you desire for your business.

Here is the thing ...

You are not instinctively born knowing how to 'do' marketing. When you train in something you love and want to share your message with others, you hit a point where you realise that the clients don't just appear. Without clarity on these areas, these are all questions blocking your way.

THINK ABOUT YOUR YOU-NIQUE BRILLIANCE

What are your best skills and talents?

What do others appreciate in you?

How do you inspire / encourage / empower others?

Where there is interest there is ability

AND THE ANSWERS CAN ALL BE FOUND IN YOUR NUMBERS.

Connecting you deeper to your message

If you are not completely clear about your message, how do you expect your clients to find you? If you speak to everyone you speak to no one.

You need to own and articulate what you do in such a way that your ideal client will hear you loud and clear and want to know more.

Which clients do you get the best results with?

Which clients are the most energetic fit for you?

Do these clients have the ability to pay what you want to charge?

Can you reach your ideal clients in large numbers?

This is where you start to build your niche, but many people fear to niche, as they think …

If I only work with women, what about men?

If I only work with men, what about women?

If I only work with over 35s – what about under 35s?

If I only work with heart-centred female business owners, what about professionals or the corporate market?

So, in line with your numbers – you need to make sure …

- You are quantifying **WHO** you work with – your ideal client / target market
- You are explaining **HOW** you help them – identifying the problem they have

- You are clarifying the **OUTCOME** of working with you – identifying the result you achieve

Clients buy if they can see the value.

When you completely **OWN** and **CONNECT** to the **BENEFITS = RESULTS** of your products and services it makes selling you products and services so much easier.

In line with your numbers ...

Think about your message – what are you currently saying?

Which transpires as ...

- I help ...   (**WHO** you are helping)
- By ...   (**HOW** you help them)
- Which means that ...   (The **RESULT** you get them).

Let's now add your magic - how you help people in accordance with your Life Path number ...

Life Path 1 - Your business message is related to ...

- Introducing others to 'never-been-done-before' projects.
- Birthing something innovative and original into the world.
- Using your initiative to individualise your character.

***Clue - I am a Life Path 1 - Bizology® is new, original and individual.

Life Path 2 - Your business message is related to ...

- Helping others create balance in their life.
- Demonstrating that you understand others' needs through your considerate nature.
- Using your powers of persuasion, diplomacy and co-operation to bring others together.

Life Path 3 - Your business message is related to ...

- Helping others by being optimistic and seeing the lighter side of life.
- Sparking people's imagination by expressing your ideas creatively.
- Using your ability to communicate - write / speak / perform / present - through every marketing platform.

Life Path 4 - Your business message is related to ...

- Showing others that their pipe dream can become a reality.
- Helping them create a plan by organising, managing and building.
- Establishing systems, order and regulation in business, by being the complete finisher.

Life Path 5 - Your business message is related to ...

- Helping others become adaptable in their lives and business.
- Using your great mental agility and versatile ability.
- By introducing new ideas and expansive methods into the world.

Life Path 6 - Your business message is related to ...

- Working together with people in groups, teaching others in a community.
- Understanding how others feel in business by showing empathy and comfort.
- Incorporating ideals of responsibility and empathy into everything you do.

Life Path 7 - Your business message is related to ...

- Sharing your wisdom and intellectual powers.
- Studying, researching, testing, proving - making sure of the facts.
- Then demonstrating your knowledge to educate others in business.

Life Path 8 - Your business message is related to ...

- Bringing people up to your level through achieving high quality standards.
- Helping others accomplish and achieve in business.
- A drive for quality and excellence in all that you do.

Life Path 9 - Your business message is related to ...

- Helping others through service over success.
- By love, compassion, tolerance, understanding and generosity.
- Through your deep interest in humanitarian endeavours.

MASTER NUMBERS 11 / 22

Life Path 11 - Your business message is related to ...

- Illuminating the truth for others using your instinctive wisdom.
- Using originality and individualisation - using the 1 energy, with the persuasive skill of 2 (as 1+1=2).
- Sharing your extraordinary insights and excellent imagination with your audiences.

Life Path 22 - Your business message is related to ...

- Using your ability to see more, be more and do more to create massive change.

- Bringing these talents together = using your skills of working with others = 2 (from the 22), to build something sustainable = 4 (2+2=4). Plus, your ability to inspire others, 2x11=22.

- Life Path Number 22s are here for big things, so the message you share is in fact bigger than you, it's part of your life's mission.

CHAPTER 14

LIFE PATH NUMBER IN BUSINESS - SOLVING PROBLEMS

I once heard a coach say, 'Your one job is to solve your ideal client's problem.' This really stuck with me.

We are in the business of solving problems, people do not buy their way into something – they buy their way out of something.

Someone who is great at solving problems is Jamie Oliver a Life Path 9 - The Humanitarian - good at seeing the bigger picture.

His market told him ... "Your recipes take too long ..." – so he gave them 'Jamie's 30 Minutes meals.'

His market then told him "30 minutes is too long; it can take that just to prepare" – so he gave them 'Jamie's 15-minute meals.'

His market then told him "There are too many ingredients" – so he came up with '5 ingredients.'

His market then told him "It is too expensive to buy these ingredients" – so he came up with 'Save with Jamie.'

His market told him "There is too much washing up" – so he came up with 'One Pan Wonders.'

Be the solution to your clients' problems. Look at the headaches that they face and create an antidote to this.

People act on emotion not logic

You need to show your ideal clients that you know how to solve their problems and that you have done this for others.

A common mistake in marketing is failing to present benefits. People buy benefits first. You need to get clear on the problems and pain points that your ideal clients have and that you have a solution to solve it.

Your ideal prospect will be asking themselves WIIFM – what's in it for me?

People are busy, your ideal client will want to know how you can help them solve their problems. What are you offering your clients? What are the benefits of the offer and what are the results?

Sell the sizzle ... not the sausage.

Your job is to show your target market that ...

1. You know their pain points = their problems.
2. You understand how this is affecting their lives and aggravating them from moving forward.
3. You have a solution that addresses their problems that will help them.

It's that simple!

However, whilst you are in the business of solving problems, the way that you do this will differ considering your Life Path number.

Let's dive deep into the world of solving your ideal client's problems in line with your numeric energies.

Solving Problems as a Life Path 1 - The Leader

- Be the antidote to people feeling stuck and needing to create the new in their business.

- By being the ultimate problem solver, helping others explore the unknown.

- You will need continually to find new audiences to share your new ideas.

Solving Problems as a Life Path 2 - The Sensitive

- Be the antidote to people feeling frustrated in their business by using your intuition to bring balance and harmony.

- By supporting and encouraging, through using your gentle persuasion.

- Helping businesses see all sides of the equation through your powers of perception and analytical ways.

Solving Problems as a Life Path 3 - The Communicator

- Be the antidote to people struggling to communicate and share their message in business.

- By bringing fresh optimism to problems by using your sharp mental skills to assess situations.

- You will find common ground with most and a subject to share with all.

Solving Problems as a Life Path 4 - The Builder

- Be the antidote to people being disorganised and scattered in their business.

- By helping to actualize ideas into tangible results, seeing the difference between wild schemes and real merit by injecting common sense.

- Creating a practical route for others to take to make their abstract concepts a reality.

Solving Problems as a Life Path 5 - The Adventurer

- Be the antidote to people feeling stale and bored in their business.

- By helping them acquire and assimilate new concepts and information.

- This includes global and international business with travel opportunities.

Solving Problems as a Life Path 6 - The Nurturer

- Be the antidote to people feeling disconnected in their business.

- By creating a tribe that people feel they can be a part of.

- You are good at reading the emotional needs of others and have the ability to help people feel cared for and supported.

Solving Problems as a Life Path 7 - The Seeker

- Be the antidote to people feeling that they are missing a piece of the important business puzzle.

- By being a specialist in your chosen subject.

- You have a knack of knowing and finding out the truth, people will gravitate towards you for this knowledge.

Solving Problems as a Life Path 8 - The CEO

- Be the antidote to people feeling their business is lacking direction, skill and strategy.

- By helping them create sustainable goals and realistic plans.

- You are balanced with a good judge of character and impartial when required.

Solving Problems as a Life Path 9 – The Humanitarian

- Be the antidote to people feeling that they are not doing enough to help others (and the planet).

- By helping them see the bigger picture and connecting them to their business vision.

- You have seen enough of life not to judge others and are good at absorbing and reflecting other people's experiences back to them.

Solving Problems as a Life Path 11 – The Spiritual Teacher

- Be the antidote to people feeling 'there must be more than this' in their business.

- By your great capacity for inspirational leadership.

- You have an original mind and a 6th sense for knowing what will work in business.

Solving Problems as a Life Path 22 – The Architect of Change

- Be the antidote to people seeking transformation in their life and business.

- By helping them create change, make improvements and make things happen.

- You are here to find ways to build a better world in business by using your abilities on a grand scale.

CHAPTER 15

LIFE PATH NUMBER IN BUSINESS
- SHOW UP, SELL AND SHINE
ON SOCIAL

One of the most important elements to your marketing strategy is visibility.

Being visible is something that business owners can struggle with, being consistent (not constant) and persistent with your marketing can be something that slips to the bottom of the pile. Running a business is THE olympics for all things personal development so being visible can be quite triggering.

There may be other people in your market doing what you do, BUT there is only one of you, using Bizology® to cut through the clutter and noise, you can become and remain visible and relevant in line with your numeric energies.

How you show up in your business is much more powerful if done in alignment with the energy of your numbers, especially when the waters seem more difficult to navigate.

One size does not fit all, so the way that one Life Path is visible on social media is very different from the next, relating your Life Path number to the best social strategy available for your numeric energies.

Placing you as a business owner and your personal energies at the centre of all your business efforts to increase impact and connection with your audience.

SW SW SW SW SW

I heard that anagram years ago and it means ...

Some will ...

Some won't ...

So what ...

Someone is watching ...

Someone is waiting.

Translated as ...

Some people will work with you.

Some people won't work with you.

So what? Stop trying to be liked by everyone - you don't even like everyone!

Someone is checking you out on your socials / website / reading your blog / listening to your podcast, RIGHT NOW and watching what you are doing.

BUT someone is waiting for the right time as timing is everything, timing is divine.

So keep showing up!

However, the way you show up, share your content and build your business will depend on the numeric energies that you are working with.

Let's look at the supercharged way your Life Path number shows up, sells and shines on social media ...

Life Path 1 – The Leader –
Show up, Sell and Shine on Social by...

Show Up ...

- Thought leadership sums up a Life Path 1, you are here to seed fresh ideas and get people thinking out of the box.

Visibility Vibes ...

- Use your innovative ability by consistently creating new content for your community to get their teeth into.

Posting style ...

- Create bitesize sales pages, social posts, blogs and stories - the energy needs to be high quick-start.

Engage by ...

- Posting little and often, use punchy, short statements that can be shared across your social platforms. You don't always like the limelight - so when you notice this make sure your content and visibility is consistent.

Watch out for ...

- Things take time, so watch your impatience. The day you plant the seed is not the day you eat the fruit. Things take time to come to fruition.

Life Path 2 – The Sensitive
Show up, Sell and Shine on Social by ...

Show Up ...

- Life Path 2 needs positive and loyal connections, feeling part of the community on the platforms you share.

Visibility Vibes ...

- Natural diplomats and quiet influencers, through persuasive talking you reach people with your words and mediation skills.

Posting style ...

- Good at attending to the details and gathering facts, you enjoy and are good at keeping abreast of online analytics.

Engage by ...

- Great at seeing both sides of the story, if there is any online drama you are quite good at smoothing the water, as long as you do not start it (by being too emotional).

Watch out for ...

- Life Path 2s need to feel supported by their surroundings, you can operate through fear, so will need to feel secure to share online.

Life Path 3 – The Communicator
Show up, Sell and Shine on Social by ...

Show Up ...

- Life Path 3s are born to put their word into the world, sharing from the online stage will come naturally.

Visibility Vibes ...

- You enjoy being at the centre of attention.

Posting style ...

- Born entertainers; you are here to add an uplifting and inspiring angle to business.

Engage by ...

- Starting conversations and lighting the match under hot topics.

Watch out for ...

- 3s don't like to be criticised and can worry about what others think of them, so watch retreating and recoiling and avoid sharing on social media because of this.

Life Path 4 – The Builder
Show up, Sell and Shine on Social by ...

Show Up ...

- The word strategy was created for Life Path 4s as 4 is about structure, control, routine and systems.

Visibility Vibes ...

- Have a plan for your content and communication strategy, you have the powers of focus and concentration to implement this.

Posting style ...

- And then it is a case of carrying this out to the letter, write a list and work through it.

Engage by ...

- Helping others build steadily and slowly, creating well laid foundations in their business.

Watch out for ...

- Be careful of being too rigid and inflexible as being visible sometimes means being available for opportunities that occur in the moment.

Life Path 5 – The Adventurer
Show up, Sell and Shine on Social by ...

Show Up ...

- 5 is about being progressive and forward thinking with your content, sharing headlines in various ways.

Visibility Vibes ...

- 'Go Big or Go Home' is the theme for Life Path 5s.

Posting style ...

- It's OK to post on the fly, if the plan is too tight or restrictive it will not work for a Life Path 5.

Engage by ...

- The operative word is change, plans will change a few times along the way and that's fine, in fact it's necessary.

Watch out for ...

- You will need flexibility with your content plan, however, be careful not to be too scattered and not have a plan. Conversely you will not like being too tied down to create pieces of content for specific dates or times.

Life Path 6 – The Nurturer
Show up, Sell and Shine on Social by ...

Show Up ...

- Lead on your business VALUES and create related content that connects to your tribe.

Visibility Vibes ...

- Relationships are important to a Life Path 6, so get visible by creating 'storytelling' content for your community.

Posting style ...

- 6 has an aesthetic side, seeing and presenting things visually. Personal branding will appeal.

Engage by ...

- Focus on the needs of those in your community and show up to help others by creating a 'tribal energy' where others also feel safe to share.

Watch out for ...

- The way you use social channels needs to be more than purely transactional (yes this can be said for all Life Path numbers BUT especially a Life Path 6 as it is about building deeper relationships).

Life Path 7 – The Seeker -
Show up, Sell and Shine on Social by ...

Show Up ...

- Through deep thought, Life Path 7 has the ability to reason using the powers of analysis.

Visibility Vibes ...

- Show up and create content in a way that is different and unique to you.

Posting style ...

- Life Path 7s love to learn – so research and development will underpin the content that you share.

Engage by ...

- Get under the bonnet of the business and share the nuts and bolts of behind the scenes. Share stats and facts - create infographics, share proof!

Watch out for ...

- You have to be careful that you do not suffer from paralysis analysis, so you will need to take space and time off the online stage to rest and retreat.

Life Path 8 – The CEO –
Show up, Sell and Shine on Social by ...

Show Up ...

- Lead with executive, professional, CEO energy (rather than the entrepreneurial style of a Life Path 1). 8 is The Boss. Goal setting is key, make sure that you factor in strategies and plans.

Visibility Vibes ...

- The information shared needs to be of high calibre and authentic to your brand.

Posting style ...

- Less is more for a Life Path 8 – create quality posts over quantity posts.

Engage by ...

- Focus on content monetization, turning your posts into profit.

Watch out for ...

- As a Life Path 8 you can be hyper critical of self (especially female 8s), so make sure this does not stop you posting.

Life Path 9 – The Humanitarian –
Show up, Sell and Shine on Social by ...

Show Up ...

- What do we do when we need help in the UK? We call 999, as 9 is about helping others.

Visibility Vibes ...

- Be clear about how the content you are sharing is adding value to your ideal clients' lives.

Posting style ...

- 9 is about the bigger picture, Life Path 9s are great at having a vision and deep down know that things are going to get done, and because of this can miss the details, so need to ensure that these get carried through.

Engage by ...

- Come from the place of a passion to help, serve and heal through the ability to empathise with your audience.

Watch out for ...

- 9s needs strong boundaries, don't give the farm away in your content, stick them on a horse and take them around the stables ☺

Life Path 11 – The Spiritual Teacher –
Show up, Sell and Shine on Social by ...

Show Up ...

- By bringing intellect and intuition into balance in your business.

Visibility Vibes ...

- Share a message that is bigger than you, by retreating from the noise of the online world in order to receive cosmic guidance.

Posting style ...

- Then when you have a vision – that is insightful and illuminates ...

Engage by ...

- You will need a plan, a direction, in order to turn the inspiration into a reality online.

Watch out for ...

- High moral standards - be careful not to impose these on others too much.

Life Path 22 – The Architect of Change – Show up, Sell and Shine on Social by ...

Show Up ...

- As a Life Path 22 you are born to share a message that is bigger than you.

Visibility Vibes ...

- Create the change you want to see in the world through your social channels, by putting your name to something, starting a movement online.

Posting style ...

- Most content created will have the scope for PR and paid ads to help engage a wider reach.

Engage by ...

- Sharing your many tests and trials in life through your transformative content.

Watch out for ...

- Limiting beliefs – get over yourself 😊 and post.

CHAPTER 16

LIFE PATH NUMBER IN BUSINESS - TIME MANAGEMENT

The two main objections people have when considering a purchase is time and money.

Have they got the time? Have they got the money?

I once saw this turned around, a coach asked, 'If this program is not for you, is it just about the time or Is it anything else?' 'Is it just about the money, or is it anything else?' Good questions, as it's easy to use time and money as an excuse not to move forward in our business, and there may be other things going on.

Let's talk about time ...

There are 24 hours in a day.

There are 1,440 minutes in a day.

There are 86,400 seconds in a day.

Of this time, you need to sleep, eat, drink, bathe, dress, manage a house, care for and communicate with family and run a business!

One of the main reasons that people cite for not acting on the things they say they want in business is due to lack of time. You can make more money, but you can't make more time.

What you can do with time is manage it. You can prioritise your time, by making things non-negotiable, being more intentional with what you spend your time on. Managing time is a choice – binge a series of Netflix or write your business book? It's your call.

The way you do this will be in relation to your numeric energies, starting with your Life Path number.

You can't magic up more hours in the day, but you can make sure you run your business from your numeric energies and this includes managing your time.

So how do you manage time in relation to your Life Path number? Let's look ...

Life Path 1 - The Leader
Will manage time in your business by ...

- Making sure you prioritise your time to anything related to doing untried things in an original way.

- Aligning your business strategies and activities to thinking, exploring, developing and planning, and then birthing new concepts.

- Ensuring the project, meeting, membership, coach, XYZ, etc is helping you achieve these things then prioritise that.

Life Path 2 - The Sensitive
Will manage time in your business by ...

- Making sure you prioritise your time to create balance.

- Pulling back to move forward when business feels a bit overwhelming. If prioritising a walk in nature helps you reconnect then this is important.

- Creating a harmonious working environment, the anagram for TEAM, 'Together Everyone Achieves More' was written for you, Life Path 2s

Life Path 3 - The Communicator
Will manage time in your business by ...

- Making sure you prioritise your time by working smart not hard. Have you heard the phrase 'Do what you do best and outsource the rest?', well this is the Modus Operandi for you Life Path 3.

- Optimising any opportunity you have to share your business message? Action this = visibility over productivity.

- Trying to avoid the 9am-5pm daily grind and create daily schedules that work well with your energy.

Life Path 4 - The Builder
Will manage time in your business by ...

- Innately knowing where to invest and allocate your time with project management.

- Making sure you prioritise implementing methodical systems, as you need order to function as a business owner.

- Establishing deep business foundations so that you can build your business to higher levels.

Life Path 5 - The Adventurer
Will manage time in your business by ...

- Making sure you prioritise your time by creating space for opportunities.

- Being reactive rather than proactive, this sounds counter intuitive, but ...

- Allowing space so that you can react in the moment and not operate from a back-to-back diary; as a Life Path 5 you will profit from this.

Life Path 6 - The Nurturer
Will manage time in your business by ...

- Making sure you prioritise your time related to opportunities to connect in networks, groups and communities.

- Building your business through relationships and affiliates, attending events and meetings where you can meet other business owners.

- Performing better in your business when your home is in order as your home is your castle.

Life Path 7 - The Seeker
Will manage time in your business by ...

- Making sure you prioritise your time to learning as 7 is about questioning, asking and analysing.

- Learning, as the more a Life Path 7 learns, the more they earn in business.

- Appreciating that you not only love space and time out from the busy business world - you categorically need this. You will also work better alone.

Life Path 8 - The CEO
Will manage time in your business by ...

- Making sure you prioritise your time to being the ultimate professional with standards of excellent calibre, wanting to give your best to everything.

- Quality over quantity – the top end of the package staircase is where we want a Life Path 8 to put their energies.

- Delegating routine work so you can work on the CEO activities.

Life Path 9 - The Humanitarian
Will manage time in your business by ...

- Making sure you prioritise your time to helping others, sounds simple but ...

- Acknowledging that a Life Path 9 can be as successful as any other number; you just need to head in the opposite direction in order to achieve this.

- Allowing for flexibility and freedom in your business, as you will get bored with one business model.

Life Path 11 - The Spiritual Teacher
Will manage time in your business by ...

- Making sure you dedicate part of your day connecting to Spirit, Source, ultimately God - this is where you get your ideas.

- Developing and trusting your intuitive response to important situations and events.

- Making sure you follow ONE clear pathway in your business at ONCE, not casting your business net too wide, as you will feel overwhelmed and ungrounded and will not achieve anything.

Life Path 22 - The Architect of Change
Will manage time in your business by ...

- Making sure you prioritise your time to creating change in the world, directing business efforts for the public good.

- Knowing that with every task you tackle - you ask yourself 'How am I achieving the above goal?'

- Ensuring you have lots of support in your business and only spend your time on things that you can do, resulting in transformation for others. Do what you do best and outsource the rest!

So that you are in control of your business and that your business is not in control of you!

CHAPTER 17

LIFE PATH NUMBER IN BUSINESS - ONE THING EACH NUMBER CAN DO DAILY TO CREATE SUCCESS

Every week in my membership, 'The Bizology® Magic Circle', https://josoley.com/bizology-magic-circle/ I have a thread where I answer the members' questions. A question that was once asked by a Magic Circler was - 'What ONE thing can each Life Path number do daily to move forward in business?' What a great question, I loved it so much that I added it into this book.

Business habits are important, so how can you hit the floor running each day in line with your numbers?

What ONE thing can you do daily, in relation to your Life Path number to move the business needle forward ...

Life Path 1 – The Leader - At the top of the day ...

- Look at your diary at the tasks and meetings you have scheduled and ask yourself, 'How are these activities dynamic and courageous in energy?'

- As 1 is all about ingenuity, the best way a Life Path 1 brings this energy into business is by ensuring that there is space to brainstorm and meet exciting new people.

- Giving the entrepreneurial flair that runs through your bones a platform. If it's Groundhog Day every day, then you will not have the creative energy you need to step forward on the stepping stones into your 'never-done-before' projects.

Life Path 2 - The Sensitive - At the top of the day ...

- Look at your diary, make sure you have space to organise and plan within your day, and ask yourself. 'Have I paid attention to all the details required to manage my time including regular breaks?' Super busy? Well, the above is even more important.

- Life Path 2s are inherently emotional; you thrive on emotional connection with others and need to feel emotionally connected to your business.

- On the flipside you can feel easily overwhelmed so ensure you are supported by your environment (flowers, essential oils, an organised desk and diary etc) and that you have space to breathe throughout the day, giving you the balance in business that you need to succeed.

Life Path 3 - The Communicator - At the top of the day ...

- Look at your diary and ask yourself – 'How am I communicating today in my business?' It is important that space is created for this. Be it a blog, a podcast, social posts, lives, writing a couple of pages of your book, leading a masterclass.

- Just watch you are sharing content of value and not ranting for the sake of it. As Life Path 3s can say, 'Let me tell you - and then they do!'

- Life Path 3s makes friends easily and will NEED to speak to people in business, having an outlet to bounce ideas off others.

Life Path 4 - The Builder - At the top of the day ...

- Look at your diary and ask yourself: 'Do I have plans and routines in place to ensure that I naturally execute my business strategy?'

- This is not the issue for Life Path 4s who are born strategists, the issue is being hyper focused with your head in your 'must-do' list that you miss opportunities that come your way, so awareness is required here.
- Schedule in regular holidays as you need to make sure you don't burn out.

Life Path 5 – The Adventurer - At the top of the day ...

- Look at your diary and ask yourself - 'Have I got scope for freedom today in my business?', you don't want to have everything planned to the 'nth degree as this will not work.
- Ensure there is space in the diary to be reactive instead of proactive. Keeping plans loose so that you can respond accordingly as Life Path 5s are faced with more opportunity in business than any other number.
- The issue with this is that you can feel scattered with so many things happening at once, not finish anything. Prioritise your top 'MIT's' - most important tasks.

Life Path 6 – The Nurturer - At the top of the day ...

- Look at your diary and ask yourself, 'How am I connecting with others to move my business forward today?'
- Life Path 6 will feel a genuine sense of accomplishment in their business when they are nurturing others.
- Days on end working alone is not where the juice happens for a 6, there needs to be collaboration, connection and relationship building.

Life Path 7 – The Seeker - At the top of the day ...

- Look at your diary and ask yourself, 'How is my diary set up to expand my business knowledge in some shape or form today?'

- Short on time? Treat yourself like a client and block an hour or two to read and gen up on the hot topics and latest news in your industry, this approach will really oil your business wheels.

- Life Path 7s are shrewd thinkers and will need to consider things carefully, so the bigger the deal, proposal, project - the more time you will need for this ... just make sure you don't overthink!

Life Path 8 - The CEO - At the top of the day ...

- Look at your diary and ask yourself, 'How am I ringing my business till today?' Shouldn't every Life Path number be asking this? Well, yes of course, but especially for a Life Path 8, as 8 is about making money.

- Life Path 8s are ninjas at goal setting, and this drives your business forward. Prioritise those IPAs (Income Producing Activity) goals.

- You have the acumen to accomplish your ambitious goals, so ensure your business has scope for this.

Life Path 9 - The Nurturer - At the top of the day ...

- Look at your diary and ask yourself, 'How am I helping people today?' Yes, all Life Path numbers help people daily as we are all in the business of solving problems, but for a Life Path 9 this is your Modus Operandi.

- It is not about the money; you can be super successful, but your focus needs to be different.

- Life Path 9s will experience changes and losses and have the ability to cope with grace with what life throws at you.

Life Path 11 – The Spiritual Teacher - At the top of the day ...

- Look at your diary and ask yourself, 'How am I using my master number and my telephone line to Spirit?', as this connection will provide the inspiration you need to share through your business.

- Life Path 11s have the ability to achieve a lot in this lifetime but will have daily tests along the way, so ensure your business has strong support systems.

- You have the exceptional ability to educate and motivate others in business if you use your gifts fully, so embrace the opportunities to do this.

Life Path 22 – The Architect of Change - At the top of the day ...

- You know the phrase 'Aim for the moon, if you miss at least you will land among the stars'. This sums up the ability of a Life Path 22 (when consciously working in the energy of 22 and not 4). Look at your diary and ask yourself, 'How can I hit the moon today?' As a master number you have all the tools to be able to do this coupled with great determination.

- As a Life Path 22, you will be in the public eye in some way, so get comfortable with being visible on a daily basis.

- You are here to improve the world by taking it by the scruff of the neck and making it better for the rest of us. What are you waiting for, Life Path 22s?

CHAPTER 18

LIFE PATH NUMBER IN BUSINESS - HOW DIFFERENT LIFE PATH NUMBERS CAN SABOTAGE THE PROCESS OF MANIFESTING

On episode 5 of my podcast, The Bizology® Soundbites - I spoke to Richard Abbot about manifesting in business and how your numeric energies can unconsciously block the flow of abundance, because controversially, manifesting can cost.

> Definition of manifesting - *'To create something or turn something from an idea into a reality. Manifestation generally means using our thoughts, feelings and beliefs to bring something to our physical reality.'*

Richard says that ... *'There is no question about it, manifesting is definitely a 'thing', everyone can do it and there is an argument to say that it is our birthright to be able to do it. The Universe, Life, is a balanced 'thing', if there is no balance it will be brought back into balance somewhere along the line. Therefore, everything we take, we need to give something in return, a universal give and take, so before we think about manifesting anything we need to understand this.'*

'Manifestation is a 'thing', but the Life Path number is also a 'thing'. We are all unique and are all here to do something unique, there is a universal plan for each of us. We can adhere to the plan or ignore it, but we all have a path we are all meant to be following. Manifesting when you are along your path is a different thing entirely than trying to manifest when you are not on your path. Numerology helps us to work out what your path is, but you can only manifest and hang onto what you are trying to manifest if it

is aligned to your Life Path - if it's not you will get it and lose it or you will not be able to get it at all.'

You can manifest what you want as long as you are willing to pay the price, however the price may not always be financial.

There is no question whether manifestation works, the question is whether we should be trying to manifest what we say we want, and this is a totally different story, a case of 'be careful what you wish for.'

In this podcast episode, Richard and I go on to discuss that a lot of people are brilliant at manifesting but not so brilliant at holding onto the things they manifest - think the infamous lottery winner stories, the abundance comes in and goes straight out. When we manifest, a common situation is that we create a supply, but can we hold onto the supply?

Real problems can occur when you are trying to manifest something that is not in alignment with the energy of your life's path. We need to be careful to examine our intentions and motivations. If your intentions are not in alignment with your Life Path number, manifesting won't work. It is therefore important to appreciate why you are trying to get XYZ? This is a crucial step in the manifestation process.

IMPORTANT***
There is a Universal plan in our lives and the only thing we should be trying to manifest is our Life Purpose, which can be seen in our numbers. Remember we do not know better than the Universal plan.

From the podcast episode with Richard, I share below some very 'top line' insights regarding the ways each Life Path number can get in its own way and block the flow when it comes to manifesting in their business.

Life Path 1   The Leader

- When it comes to manifesting in business, Life Path 1s must get onboard with the fact that abundance comes from the Universe, the divine and not you, as a Life Path 1 you are used to doing everything for yourself.

- Entrepreneurship, self-employment has to happen in order for manifestation to happen, as manifesting supports your path and the path Life Path 1 supports is independence.

- So a Life Path 1 can never come into its own by working for someone else. Abundance, success, fulfilment will come to a Life Path 1 when you are working for yourself.

Life Path 2   The Sensitive

- When it comes to manifesting in business, Life Path 2s must let go of fear. In order to manifest you need to be willing to be transformed by the process of manifesting, and for Life Path 2s this means moving past fear in order to grow.

- If you do not grow and stay in the energy of fear, it will be tricky to manifest what you say you desire.

- Life Path 2s need to let go of fear to open themselves up to be able to attract the possibilities that are available to them through manifesting.

Life Path 3   The Communicator

- When it comes to manifesting in business, Life Path 3s like nice things and these things can cost money. 3s have the ability to spend, spend, spend, this in itself is a block. Abundance goes to abundance; money goes to money. Money does not go to zero money, Life Path 3s are good at going to zero in their bank account due to their desire to spend.

- Look at the shape of the 3, it is made up of 2 horseshoes. Life Path 3s are lucky, Kylie Minogue is a 3 and she sings 'I should be so lucky!' Kylie is correct but luck can run out. 3 energy can be, 'I want this now, so I will get it now.'

- In light of this 3s are good at manifesting things but not so good at holding on to them, so need to start the manifesting process again. It is then hard to get things moving as 3s are impatient waiting for things to happen. What are you actually trying to manifest and what are you going to do with it when you get it? Remember if you disrespect money it disrespects you back. This is something a 3 is here to learn.

Life Path 4   The Builder

- When it comes to manifesting in business, Life Path 4s tend to get stuck.

- Abundance wants to move. 4 can operate from a lack mindset and focus on hoarding resources and this is not the right vibration to manifest.

- Life Path 4s can be rigid and controlling, the energy of manifestation needs to flow, so Life Path 4s will need to release control to allow this flow.

Life Path 5   The Adventurer

- When it comes to manifesting in business, 5 is the number of change but also the number of loss. You can't win if you are not prepared to lose.

- With Life Path 5 money will come in and go out, if you try to hold on to everything then you will lose everything.

- In order to manifest a given thing, 5s have to identify that thing, which means identifying what that thing is not.

Manifestation requires focus and concentration, saying yes to this and no to that. 5s can want success in 20 different areas, but this is unlikely to work as your energy is spread too thinly in the manifestation process.

Life Path 6   The Nurturer

- When it comes to manifesting in business 6 is a giving number rather than a receiving number, so Life Path 6 can find it hard to manifest.

- 6 is about 'We' not 'I', if 6 can be convinced that the goal is good for 'We' - them and their children / family / business / community / society, etc, then 6s can manifest. If there is any lingering doubt the '6' energy will get in the way and will not allow the manifestation process to work.

- If you believe what you desire will help others then you will be able to get on board the manifesting train, but you will need to see a collective energy and result in your efforts, not just make it about you.

Life Path 7   The Seeker

- When it comes to manifesting in business Life Path 7s are actually not often interested in abundance and success. The material world distracts a 7 from who they really are. 8 is the number of accumulation and abundance and you are not the number next to you.

- The most aligned thing a Life Path 7 can manifest would be related to knowledge, for example, admission to a course, as the more they learn the more they earn, but it has to be this way around, learning first then earning.

- If a Life Path 7 can see what they are manifesting allows

them to learn, they will be able to activate the manifesting process, but they will need to be able to see a higher reason for it.

Life Path 8   The CEO

- When it comes to manifesting in business Life Path 8s can be too specific with regards to what success looks like, and this can block the flow of manifestation.

- As an 8, you can be perfectionists and have defined details of what you desire, giving the Universe too much work to do and straining its powers, taking a job that is not that easy and making it harder.

- Life Path 8s can manifest but can end up paying a bigger price for it. By being too specific with desires you can discard the possibilities available to you, not allowing leeway for magic to happen, narrowing down the chance of the Universe bringing it to you.

Life Path 9   The Humanitarian

- When it comes to manifesting in business Life Path 9s are very emotional, so you have to want what you are seeking from an emotional stance.

- During the manifestation process, you can't be lukewarm about your goals, or feel guilty about them, as the vibration of Life Path 9 is to serve others not self.

- If you don't really want it, you won't get it, and one of the negatives of 9 is your inability to deserve.

Life Path 11 and Life Path 22
The Spiritual Teacher / The Architect of Change

- When it comes to manifesting in business Life Path 11s and Life Path 22s have the ability to be master manifestors, but you will need to understand, control and activate your master number energy for manifestation to take place. Master numbers can be accidental manifestors!

- You will need to examine your motivations deeply, know what you are trying to get, know why you are trying to get it and appreciate the consequences of what is going to happen when you do manifest what you say you want.

- The barrier to manifestation with master numbers can be negative self-talk, self-sabotaging by getting in one's own way. Manifestation takes place in cooperation with the Universe and master numbers need to surrender to this, instead of powering through with their own energy. 'Let Go, Let God' and sometimes master numbers do not want to do this. Spend and God will send ☺

CHAPTER 19

LIFE PATH NUMBER IN BUSINESS - THE RESILIENCE OF YOUR NUMBERS

During these intense and uncertain times which we find ourselves in (which let's face it are only going to get more intense) it is very important that we understand ourselves more than ever.

Knowing our numbers can assist us during times of crisis, so that we understand how to manage stress and even strive in times of stress, helping us to be more resilient.

Below I share tips to help you become stronger and more adaptable when life is difficult to navigate ...

Resilient tips if you are working with the energy of the number ...

Life Path 1   The Leader

- When it comes to resilience, Life Path 1s are very independent and have unique coping strategies.

- Out of all the Life Path numbers you are able to stand alone when required.

- When life gets tricky, make your life and business about you, ignore the outside noise, put your head down and get on with what you know you need to do.

- Life Path 1 can be a lonely road, but you work best alone and have an innate power to concentrate.

- Use your inner strength to help others during times of crisis, they will look to you to lead as when push comes to shove, you are a force to be reckoned with.

Life Path 2   The Sensitive

- When it comes to resilience, Life Path 2s needs to start by creating an environment that supports you. Manage your diary, get in nature, sense check who you have in your inner circle, so you feel nourished.

- Reach out to others, 2s need interaction, even if it is virtual.

- When the chips are down you are good at making sure the show is running smoothly (as long as you keep your emotions in check and don't go into panic mode).

- Life Path 2s are surprisingly stubborn, so don't underestimate your own abilities. You are not a pushover, there is a strength of a lion in there when you need it.

- If all else fails - keep striving for balance and moderation.

Life Path 3   The Communicator

- When it comes to resilience, Life Path 3s need to keep talking, reaching out to others and sharing through all marketing mediums.

- Life Path 3s have the ability to speak and inspire others during difficult times. You make a great MC, just make sure you avoid cynicism and sarcasm.

- To do this, keep your spirits and your head high, as when you feel down it is hard to get you back up again.

- Humour really is your best medicine.

- An important point is that you don't like criticism but will attract this more than any other Life Path number especially during uncertain times. Manage the trap of 'comparitinitis', by filtering your social media and unfollowing accounts when you know you need to.

Life Path 4   The Builder

- When it comes to resilience, Life Path 4s need security in their life and business.

- When things get tough, work steadily and avoid taking any risks.

- Write a plan of action and work through it, don't make it up as you go along.

- 4s are not scared of hard work, create structure and systems in order to build for the future so that you can sustain difficult times.

- The issue for a Life Path 4 will be overworking, so ensure you have the space to implement self-care.

Life Path 5   The Adventurer

- When it comes to resilience, Life Path 5s need freedom and change - the need to mix things up and shake the business bag.

- Excitement will keep you on your business toes and your natural curiosity alight.

- You will dislike any restraint, ensure to find variety in every day, creating frequent changes of scenery.

- During times of crisis make sure you don't become too scattered by your efforts.

- Get yourself overseas when you can, as 5 is about international travel.

Life Path 6   The Nurturer

- When it comes to resilience, as Life Path 6s are the ultimate nurturers, make sure not to pile too much on your plate during rocky times.

- 6s are good listeners, and your community will acknowledge this, continue to reach out and build your audience, they need you and you need them more than ever.

- Create and maintain a peaceful home and work environment around you as much as possible and serve your tribe from this space.

- You are forgiving of others and are understanding when things do not work out or when others are going through a tough time.

- However, Life Path 6 does have a stubborn streak - so use this when necessary.

Life Path 7   The Seeker

- When it comes to resilience, Life Path 7s are the business loners, not a bad thing you are good on your own but reach out to others when required (will need to do this less than other numbers, apart from maybe Life Path 1).

- You will need space and solitude to think things through when times are challenging BUT do not procrastinate too much.

- Get in nature to recharge your business batteries.

- Trust your gut - you are innately intuitive; your first instincts will be very accurate.

- Your dry sense of humour will keep you going in times of adversity.

Life Path 8   The CEO

- When it comes to resilience, Life Path 8s are strong characters, so you will be called during times of crisis to lead and help others to rise.

- You nail it in business, 8s intuitively know what to do.

- When high standards and professionalism are called for, this is what you stand for.
- Life Path 8s are powerful people with a toughness of character, an air of authority and calmly ruthless when they have to be.
- Avoid self-recrimination during tough times.

Life Path 9   The Humanitarian

- When it comes to resilience for a Life Path 9 look at the 9th Major Arcana card in the Tarot, 'The Hermit', the light in the lantern shines the way for others, so be mindful where you take people as they will follow you.
- Life Path 9s are very old souls, energetically you will feel times of crisis very deeply.
- Yes, you are here to serve others, but make sure you implement self-care and fill your cup up first so that you do not wear yourself out in the process.
- You like to see the best in everyone but spend your compassion wisely and be careful with who you surround yourself with.
- Your intuition is rarely wrong - learn to trust this, it will keep you in good stead when the path is unknown.

Life Path 11   The Spiritual Teacher

- When it comes to resilience, Life Path 11s will need to connect upwards during challenging times, to gain incredible insight and share these messages to empower your tribe.
- When push comes to shove 11s can have great strength of character and are capable of exceptional performance.
- However as 11 is a master number and an intense energy you will need to learn how to relax, your home life will need

to be stable.

- You are incredibly intuitive but can be very emotional, so will need a plan to cope in times of crisis, balance in everything is vital.

- Remember not to take things too personally.

Life Path 22   The Architect of Change

- When it comes to resilience, as a Life Path 22 you have huge personal power, great determination and can accomplish anything you desire.

- What are you doing to create change for your global community during tough times?

- Rely on the first impressions you get with people and situations.

- Others will not grasp things as quickly as you, so watch your tolerance levels.

- However, mindset is everything - and you will need to work on this to move forward.

CHAPTER 20

LIFE PATH NUMBER IN BUSINESS - THE NEMESIS OF YOUR NUMBERS

When I work with my clients through my 121 Bizology® sessions, we look at the negatives and the challenges of their numbers, as when they understand these, and they stop playing out they can consciously work in the positives of their numbers.

This is actually the starting point. I have regular Bizology® dates with myself where I remind myself of the shadow side of my numbers, as these are the things that can trip me up in business and stop me from creating the business I desire. These are the pitfalls and stumbling blocks that, if we are honest with ourselves, make a huge difference.

One of the things I say to my clients before they embark on a Bizology® package with me is 'I need you to be really honest with yourself, not with me - but with you, because essentially we are the negatives of our numbers ...'

If you can be honest with yourself, you will see that you have these tendencies. If when you read the below there is some resistance to these areas; then maybe you need to read them again. Another way of looking at this is that each Life Path number will have a business nemesis to deal with.

Let's look at these for each Life Path number, so that you can appreciate the negatives and navigate the nemesis with awareness ...

Life Path 1   The Leader

The 1 energy = dynamic and exciting, the word impossibility does not exist.

You are a born trailblazer and are here to act with bravery to take calculated risks in business.

However ...

Business Nemesis = Lack of self-belief, can prevent Life Path 1s from trying to create the impossible.

Remember ...

- Be mindful of being self-centred and selfish - it's not always about you ... you will need to learn to listen to advice.

- Watch your speed and impatience - the day you plant the business seed is not the day you eat the business fruit.

- Be careful not to burn out, working until you are exhausted.

Life Path 2   The Sensitive

The 2 energy = has the gift of being peacemakers in business.

You are born to be the power behind the throne, you have the ability to cooperate, and are the glue that holds everything and everyone together.

However... ...

Business Nemesis = Can operate from lack, fear and panic.

Remember ...

- Watch constantly changing your mind and being flaky in business.

- Life Path 2 can be unpredictable, where do others stand with you?

- Easily hurt as you feel things deeply, can be ultra-sensitive and worry for the sake of worrying about everything.

Life Path 3   The Communicator

The 3 energy = is charming, life and soul of the business party.

You are born to shine bright – YOU will be at the heart of your business.

However …

Business Nemesis = Criticism of self and others.

Remember...

- Remember 3s can go 2 ways - some overshare and some are really uncomfortable with communication - what side of the fence are you on?

- Watch those business expenses - 3s love to spend money and they can.

- Can also have a lazy streak - be mindful of this.

Life Path 4   The Builder

The 4 energy = is solid, honest and reliable.

You are born to be the systems person who appreciates the exact steps it takes to get from A to Z.

However …

Business Nemesis = Patterns of rigid behaviour, being resistant to change.

Remember ...

- Be mindful not to be too serious.

- Not to obsess over detail.

- All work and no play makes a Life Path 4 a dull business owner.

Life Path 5   The Adventurer

The 5 energy = Dynamic freedom seeker.

You are born to learn new things and reinvent old business ways to create new exciting and intriguing enterprises.

However ...

Business Nemesis = Being jack of all trades and master of none.

Remember ...

- Can have a sense of restlessness with business. Life Path 5s need freedom but not too much freedom, being careful this does not turn to escapism or excess.
- Careful not to have too many irons in the fire and flit from one project to the next without completing anything.
- Can conversely fear change and remain stagnant.

Life Path 6   The Nurturer

The 6 energy = is dutiful and loyal.

- You are born a nurturer and naturally take responsibility for everything you do.

However ...

Business Nemesis = Interfering where you are not needed, you do not know best all the time.

Remember ...

- Can have a jealous streak - watch this in business by staying in your lane and keeping your side of the road clean.
- You sometimes like a short-cut - remember these do not exist in business.
- If 'family' is in crisis a 6 can be in crisis and then the business is put on the back burner - make sure you have a check on this. (I have seen it happen often with Life Path 6.)

Life Path 7   The Seeker

The 7 energy = have a refined and intelligent mind.

You are born a font of wisdom.

However ...

Business Nemesis = Isolation (not just during a pandemic).

Remember ...

- You can have a tendency to reflect instead of taking action; try not to hyper analyse every single thing.
- Your need for privacy can lead to secrecy in business.
- Watch your defensive streak.

Life Path 8   The CEO

The 8 energy = The crème de la crème.

You are born the ultimate manager and executive.

However ...

Business Nemesis = Only seeing things through the lens of money, resulting in greed.

Remember ...

- Watch your 'bossy' streak which is sometimes advantageous in business does not veer into aggression.
- Make sure you live and let live in business.
- Can conversely fear success.

Life Path 9   The Humanitarian

The 9 energy = Wise, kind and good at seeing the bigger picture.

You are born a creative philanthropist.

However ...

Business Nemesis = Naively thinking everyone has good intentions - they don't!

Remember ...

- Will need to focus - Life Path 9s can be daydreamers in business.
- Be careful not to want to be liked by everyone by sacrificing self.
- Life Path 9s can go either way - by either having no boundaries or refusing to help others and be very selfish.

Life Path 11   The Spiritual Teacher

The 11 energy = Inspirational and intuitive.

You are born to be the Spiritual illuminator.

However ...

Business Nemesis = Experience extremes of emotions.

Remember ...

- Master numbers are testing numbers to work with, 11 is an intense and extreme energy.
- Can be rebellious and have a temper - watch this is not used for the sake of it.
- So connected to the higher realm that will need to learn how to live in the real world.

Will need to work at activating your Life Path 11 and not work in the energy of 2.

Life Path 22   The Architect of Change

The 22 energy = Business achievement can have a very humanitarian side.

You are born to implement structures that create lasting change for others.

However ...

Business Nemesis = Self-sabotage - taking a sledgehammer to situations.

Remember ...

- Can be at war with yourself, as 22 can be a stubborn and disruptive force, get out of your own way and manage your own enterprise, that is here for the long run.
- Can be highly strung as you possess so much energy.
- Be careful not to micro-management your team.

Will need to work at activating your Life Path 22 and not work in the energy of 4.

CHAPTER 21

LIFE PATH NUMBER IN BUSINESS - 3 THINGS YOU NEED TO KNOW ...

So far in this book I have explained what the Life Path number is, how to calculate the Life Path number correctly and described the titles and energies of the Life Path numbers.

We have then gone deeper with the Life Path number and how to use it in business and I have connected you to, The Basics, Key Lessons, Your Business Strategy Unlocked, Solving Problems, Creating Your Business Message, Show Up, Sell And Shine On Social, Time Management, One Thing Each Number Can Do Daily To Create Success, How Different Numbers Can Sabotage The Process Of Manifesting, The Resilience Of Your Numbers and The Nemesis Of Your Numbers.

To round up this part of the book I am going to summarise '3 Things You Need To Know Related To Your Life Path Number ...'

You know you are a Life Path Number 1 - The Leader
So what? What do you do with this information?

1. **ALWAYS** take the self-employment route, as you hate being told what to do.

2. **LOOK** for opportunities to initiate and lead projects, it's your superpower.

3. **WATCH** your self-doubt, it will hold you back, being mindful not to lose courage or make U-turns in business.

You know you are a Life Path Number 2 - The Sensitive
So what? What do you do with this information?

1. **EMBRACE** working with others in partnership and collaboration.

2. **ACCEPT** that it can take you some time to reach decisions in business as you like to weigh everything up.

3. **NEVER** ever go against your intuition in business – if something feels off it is.

You know you are a Life Path Number 3 - The Communicator
So what? What do you do with this information?

1. **PUT** your word into the world.

2. **WORK** smart not hard, ensure you enter into things with a light approach.

3. **LEARN** how to manage your business expenses as 3s love to spend money.

You know you are a Life Path Number 4 - The Builder
So what? What do you do with this information?

1. **WRITE** a list – create a plan and work through it.

2. **PUT** your head down to achieve your precise business goals.

3. **AT** times let go and release control, being flexible and changing course when needed.

You know you are a Life Path Number 5 - The Adventurer
So what? What do you do with this information?

1. **ACTIVELY** look for adventure in your business – responding well to opportunities that are presented to you.

2. **PUSH** the boundaries and show others it is ok to do the same.

3. **TAKE CARE** to not juggle too many projects at once, achieving nothing.

You know you are a Life Path Number 6 - The Nurturer
So what? What do you do with this information?

1. **FIND** your business tribe and love them hard.

2. **HAVE** clarity on your business values and run your business from the essence of them.

3. **MONITOR** and evaluate how much responsibility you put on your business plate.

You know you are a Life Path Number 7 - The Seeker
So what? What do you do with this information?

1. **SEEK,** ask, question, analyse, learn - and then bring your findings into your business to help others.

2. **TAKE** time out to reflect on what you want for and from your business.

3. **WATCH** the energy of procrastination through analysis paralysis.

You know you are a Life Path Number 8 - The CEO
So what? What do you do with this information?

1. **NEVER** dim your ambition, keep it alight.

2. **ALIGN** to the power of perseverance because you will be tested through stormy waters.

3. **APPRECIATE** that although you are here to master the art of success through money and status, be careful not to lose sight of what really matters.

You know you are a Life Path Number 9 - The Humanitarian
So what? What do you do with this information?

1. **DON'T** forget you are here to give back and make the world a better place.

2. **REMEMBERING** not to lose yourself in the process and give too much – watch those boundaries.

3. **BE** conscious of what you need to release and let go of in order to constantly welcome the new and creative in your business.

You know you are a Life Path Number 11 - The Spiritual Teacher
So what? What do you do with this information?

1. **CONNECT** to a source higher than you and impart this knowledge – you are the Spiritual Teacher.

2. **BE** sure to have a plan and a direction, watching your tendency to delude yourself in the process.

3. **SEEK** to know – but make sure you take time out and implement a strong self-care routine.

You know you are a Life Path Number 22 - The Architect of Change
So what? What do you do with this information?

1. **BUILD** an empire that will help serve humanity one person at a time.

2. **TAP** into that huge vision, when you think you have thought big – think even bigger.

3. **WATCH** that 4 – Most 22s work in 4 – as this is easier as 2+2=4, so make sure you get past any mindset issues (and ego) to access the 22 energy. This Life Path number is a testing incarnation, you will face setbacks and challenges, but the good news is that you can totally deal with them.

CHAPTER 22

WHY COMPATIBILITY OF NUMBERS IS A REAL THING

You are not the number next to you

Compatibility is a real thing in numerology, some numbers are naturally drawn to each other, some numbers have a magnetic rapport and some numbers connect on a deeper level.

This plays out with Bizology®, your relationships with your team, business partners, affiliates, suppliers, members of your community etc. You will find it a lot easier to be on the same page with some Life Path numbers than with others.

It is important to say that this does not mean that you cannot work with, connect with or be in a business relationship with certain numbers. Some relationships will gel, some will flow and some will feel a bit tricker, depending on the person's core values and traits which are also present in the Life Path number.

When you understand the target energies of all numbers you can then appreciate why you may approach things from a different viewpoint and in turn give others and the relationship itself a bit of a break.

A good way to explain this is to look at the phrase, 'At 6s and 7s.' This phrase suggests that someone feels at odds. This perfectly describes 'You are not the number next to you as …'

6 is about relationships, responsibility, connection, love, togetherness, family and community.

7 is about learning, thinking, seeking, questioning, asking, analysing and spending time alone.

Life Path 6s need to connect with others to thrive.

Life Path 7s need their own space to thrive.

At 6s and 7s' is an idiom used to describe a condition of confusion or disarray, the two numbers are very different in energy.

Knowing you are not the number next to you is so powerful, helping us work with instead of against the energies in our relationships.

This also applies within a person. If you are a Life Path 6 and born on the 7th or 16th or 25th - there can be conflicting energies at play. The path of your life is to be 6 - The Nurturer, but the way you approach this (see Chapter 32) is 7 - The Seeker. Knowledge is power, understanding these differences can help you ensure both energies are used in your life and business instead of creating internal conflict.

Numeric relationship compatibility is not 100% accurate, there will always be grey areas, as we are all made up of a cocktail of numbers AND we all have free will, this also impacts the relationship between Life Path numbers.

Birds of a feather flock together, you will find that you gravitate towards certain numbers and that there will be a few of one certain Life Path number in your circle. As a Life Path 1, I work well with Life Path 9s and have many in my friendship group and community, as 1 and 9 complete a circle.

Odd numbers tend to get on well with odd numbers - these are numbers of the mind. Even numbers tend to get on well with even numbers - these are emotional numbers. It then goes deeper from here.

Some numbers work on a similar wavelength ...

- These relationships are harmonious, connections flow with ease.

- 3, 6, 9 is a compatible triangle as these are creative consciousness energies.

- Practical numbers and business numbers tend to gel - for example Life Paths 1, 4 and 8.

Some numbers can be super compatible or completely neutral ...

Think of the phrase, 'reason, season or lifetime', some numbers can team up to create a goal then go separate ways.

Some numbers can clash ...

Challenged to see the world from a new perspective, some numbers have much to learn and teach each other. When they come together and accept differences they can grow, this doesn't mean the connection and relationship is bad, just trickier, more effort will be required.

Two of the same Life Path numbers can be challenging - as they will both want to do the same energy of the same thing. For example, two Life Path 1s need to both put themselves first, but if two people are doing this then there is too much emphasis on their own needs. Two Life Path 4s can create a situation where they will both feel too tied down, being obsessed with detail. Two Life Path 9s will feel overwhelmed with giving and unable to recognise their own needs. The energy of the Life Path number is therefore amplified to the extreme.

Relationships are not meant to be easy, and they are one of the ways that we learn about ourselves. We all need different things and we are all here to learn different things. Our energies have different requirements. We can sometimes be so affronted and even upset that people are different, but we are all unique, we are meant to be. Accepting that people are unique is important. By looking at someone's numeric energy this helps you appreciate how they are different by understanding what they are here to learn, navigate and work with this lifetime.

Our greatest teachers challenge us the most and this is essential to our soul growth and evolution. Our uniqueness helps with our growth which helps with our business growth, and how we show up and help other people.

So topline the target energies of the numbers and what they are here to work with in business ...

1 energy is here to work and focus on ...	Self-employment and Independence
2 energy is here to work and focus on ...	Sensitivity and Balance
3 energy is here to work and focus on ...	Communication and Creativity
4 energy is here to work and focus on ...	Determination and Discipline
5 energy is here to work and focus on ...	Change and Travel
6 energy is here to work and focus on ...	Relationships and Community
7 energy is here to work and focus on ...	Learning and Introspection
8 energy is here to work and focus on ...	Success and Professionalism
9 energy is here to work and focus on ...	Compassion and Charity
11 energy is here to work and focus on ...	Inspiration and Illumination
22 energy is here to work and focus on ...	Transformation and Change making

Take a look at the target energies, the energy next to each other is very different. Work out the Life Path numbers of the people in your personal and business life (using the Life Path calculation I provided you with in Chapter 8) or use my free Life Path app here https://josoley.com/LIFE-PATH-APP/ to see the energies you are both working with.

The detail pertaining to which Life Path number gets on with which in business is a deeper subject which I cover in my Bizology® 121 sessions, this also goes deeper depending how in sync your Personal Years are. In Bizology® Teams, we also look at your team's numbers and compatibility, highlighting where deeper attention to the relationship is needed. Like anything - awareness is key in relationships.

CHAPTER 23

4 TRICKY NUMBERS · KARMIC DEBT

There are 4 testing numbers that are also referred to as Karmic Debt numbers. A lot of people panic when they hear this term, no number is 'bad', however some numbers are 'tricky' meaning they face difficulties and challenges.

> **Definition of Karma** *'The sum of a person's actions in this and previous states of existence, viewed as deciding their fate in future existences.'*

If you have a Karmic number in your numeric chart, it highlights what you are here to learn and work with this lifetime. As we are here to learn, life is for learning. Knowledge of Karmic Debt numbers helps us to work with its energy and manage it more effectively. If you have Karmic Debt and understand why, there are gifts available to you, life seems to make a bit more sense.

I didn't used to mention Karmic Debt numbers outside my client sessions or my membership, 'The Bizology® Magic Circle'. However, it is important to have a conversation around these numbers transparently, without fear and up front.

All 4 Karmic Debt numbers are about awareness of the need to be selfless. If you have a Karmic Debt and act mindfully with the energy of helping others then success will come. If you act selfishly then a tricky road is ahead.

Karma is just about balance. If you took in a previous life, you come back this lifetime to give back. Karmic numbers indicate inherited lessons, burdens, weaknesses and specific areas of growth that have been passed on from your previous lives that you are here to work with and address in this lifetime. So that you can master the unlearnt lesson.

The Karmic lesson will repeat itself until you resolve it. Each number has its own unique lessons and burdens. Understanding these lessons can help us step into our power and learn. Shedding a light on the places we need to pay attention to, helping us reflect, learn and grow. Testing and triggering us, like all lessons. When we learn we lessen the energy.

There are 4 key Karmic Debt numbers ...

19/10/1

13/4

14/5

16/7

Where can Karmic Debt be found?

- The Life Path Number = strongest energy it will be found.
- Day of the month you are born on – still present but not as strong as the Life Path number.
- Personal Years – you will feel the energy if you are in one of these years.
- In your Name (however your name can be changed).
- In your Business energies - it's Life Path and name.

When I show someone during a Bizology® session that they have Karmic Debt in their chart, they know on some level that this is the case. If it is in the Life Path number, they definitely know that they have been born with a monkey on their back. They acknowledge that they are here to work with deep rooted issues. Awareness is the key to change, with this understanding they can then move forward on their business path, doing something about it, repaying the debt.

Let's explore them and how they play out ...

Karmic Debt 19/10/1

How the numbers show in your chart

The 19th Major Arcana card in the Tarot is the Sun - what happens if you are in the Sun for too long or without SPF protection? You get burnt.

19 is the number of Saturn, the collector of taxes, it will demand measure for measure. If you are working with the energy of 19/10/1, in a previous life you would have acted in a selfish manner, so in this lifetime you will need to pay back to others with your time and money. In this lifetime there most likely will be a sense of frustration due to inability to control everything and everyone in your life. You will need to learn to take others' needs and feelings into consideration rather than just your own. Can also have extreme difficulty standing on your own two feet and will need to master how to do this.

Opportunity for transformation in business comes through ...

Having the courage to accept assistance from others. Admitting your mistakes. Seeing others' points of view (regardless of right or wrong). Developing selflessness and broadening your perspective. Involvement in charity or healing work. Avoiding being hyper focused, narrow minded and selfish.

***In fact, I am working with this number, life was difficult for a long time before I realised I was not only a Life Path 1, but a 19/10/1 - so although I am here to be independent, this was not natural for me. Most Life Path 1s can make their lives about them, however as a 19/10/1, if I did this my life would definitely not work so I have to make sure that I am also paying back, a delicate balance I am now aware to navigate.

Karmic Debt 13/4
How the numbers show in your chart

The 13th Major Arcana card in the Tarot is the Death card, when I pull the Death card, I see it as a chance for transformation. The number 13 is globally widely feared, at the Last Supper 13 were present - Judas deceived Jesus, who then died. Anciently 13 was a highly revered number but considered holy and unapproachable so people panicked about it. If you get in a lift in Italy the numbering will be 12, 12A then 14, avoiding 13. Nowadays there are superstitions around the number 13 and people actively avoid it. It can however be a case of 'lucky for some', people born on the 13th say this to me!

There is a warning with 13, 1+3=4= indicating laziness in a previous life. The need this lifetime will be to step away from triviality into constructive work. Extra effort is required to master discipline, integrity and determination in life and business. Learning to be responsible and facing challenges and limitations head on rather than looking for quick fixes or short-cuts.

Opportunity for transformation in business comes through ...

Applying honesty, patience and perseverance through adversity. Developing the ability to work hard within the restrictions that are imposed on your life. Avoiding the need for shortcuts, quick fixes or fast tracks, too much speculation or risk taking.

Karmic Debt 14/5
How the numbers show in your chart

The 14th Major Arcana card in the Tarot is Temperance which is about moderation and balance. 14/5 is about misusing freedom in a previous life. Also called the number of Mars, it can be destructive.

It can be difficult for 14/5 to remember. Deeply absorbed in the senses, focused on physical sensations and temptations. Indicates a need to display temperance and moderation in life and business. Being mindful of over-indulgence. Rising above temptation in favour of responsibility.

Opportunity for transformation in business comes through …

Balancing an innate desire for freedom and adventure. Developing the ability to honour your commitments, keeping diaries and lists. Demonstrating patience, moderation, tolerance and kindness. Avoiding crazes, mania, sensory overload, distractions and extremes of all kinds.

Karmic Debt 16/7
How the numbers show in your chart

The 16th Major Arcana card in the Tarot is the Tower. The one card in the pack that you may be tempted to quickly put back if you draw it! The Tower card is about upheaval and crisis. Working with 16/7 Karmic Debt creates an identity crisis within the person. You will experience tests of faith and optimism experiencing broken dreams. In life you will rise to fall, love to lose, hold to let go.

Opportunity for transformation in business comes through …

The need to re-evaluate core values by eliminating anything superficial. Learning to be responsible and facing challenges head on, rising above ego and pride, treating others with respect.

Focusing on personal development. Being honest and faithful in love. Developing Spiritual and Psychic ability. Resilience in the face of shocks. Avoiding focusing on wealth, status and titles.

If you do not have any Karmic numbers in your deeper numeric chart, it doesn't mean your life and business will be a bed of roses, there will still be challenges, and these challenges will be apparent from the negatives and nemesis of the main numeric energies in your chart.

CHAPTER 24

5 WAYS YOU COULD BE LEAVING MONEY ON THE TABLE NOT KNOWING YOUR LIFE PATH NUMBER ...

During the Coronavirus pandemic in 2020 we all had a bit more time on our hands to reflect, during this time I reflected on parts of my life, career and business. I reflected on my past, the good, the bad and the ugly. I contemplated some experiences that I may not be so proud of, wondering why they happened. 'When you lose, don't lose the lesson', it is important to realise why these things played out so we can learn from them.

When I looked at the tricker situations of my life, it boiled down to one thing - not knowing my numeric energies. In every sticky situation I was working in the negative of my numbers, against my numbers, against the energy of the Personal Year I was in and against who I am at soul level. Against what I am here to do in the world.

Now I know my numeric energies, it is interesting that these issues are not occurring as I understand who I am and what and how I am meant to be doing life and business.

A lot of people in the online coaching space talk about healing and trauma. If we are human, we will have trauma, it is a real thing and can block you from moving forward. However, if we are not careful, we can stay in perpetual healing, as we are never done, we will never get to the end of our healing journey.

A way to help us move forward is to embrace the concept of learning. The most important thing that we can learn about is ourselves. If we know who we are, the emphasis is on awareness more than trauma and healing.

Knowing your numbers gives you the awareness to help you make the most of yourself in your business so that you do not leave money on the table. Let's take a look ...

1. Don't try to be all things to all people

'Get Big, Get Niche or Get Out.' There is so much noise online, we are subjected to 175% more information than our Grandparents generation ever were. In light of this, the power of the niche is a real thing. Since understanding the energies of my numbers, I have carved a niche for myself, and confidently stand in this niche because my numbers support it.

Bringing a discipline such as Numerology into the world of business coaching has been born from a place of understanding my numbers. Literally giving me the permission to stand in my niche and it is working for me and my bottom line. In line with your numeric energies there will be a niche for you too. Remember no niche is too small if it's yours.

2. Don't put others on a pedestal

I was so very guilty of doing this, people pleasing and looking to others for all the answers. I now know my numbers hold the answers. I suffered from 'comparitinitis' and imposter syndrome. Firstly, we never ever know what someone is actually going through and if their life and business is working as well as it looks through the filtered lens of social media (and I very much doubt it is), then they are not making any mistakes, and it is through mistakes that we learn.

Understanding yourself through the lens of numerology helps you trust yourself, the process of life and the journey you are on. Helping you build your business from a place of authenticity and integrity.

3. Do you really understand who you are?

From trying to serve all of the people all of the time, looking at what other people were doing and comparing myself to them I had completely lost myself. When I left University in the 1990s I was full of optimism, vitality and excitement for my future, nothing could stop me.

25 years later I felt quite jaded from life. I'd had experiences I did not understand, relationships that hadn't worked and was running a business as a solo-preneur as I knew I had to be self-employed, but I wasn't using all my skills and talents.

Fast forward a few years I feel confident in who I am, who I am here to serve and have the energy and focus to put my head down and make it happen. As knowing my numbers increases my numbers!

4. Are you following your business purpose?

As I have shown you throughout this book, the main number we work with is our Life Path number - the path we are destined here to walk in our life and business. There are numbers that help us navigate this Life Path. There are numbers that you are ultimately aspiring to be. There are numbers that feel familiar, but you don't need to spend time being as you have already experienced it in a previous life (however much you may fancy it).

This understanding and knowledge, when translated into your business purpose and potentiality, is potent. All the gold, magic and juice are found in these numbers. Nothing else is needed.

In my deeper numeric chart, I am working with the energies of ...

1   The Leader
4   The Builder

8   The CEO
9   The Humanitarian
22   The Architect of Change.

Forget a stuffy business plan, this is my business treasure map which enables me to focus on my business cash flow, income and profit.

Showing everyone their full numeric chart is what I show my clients in their 121 Bizology® sessions.
https://josoley.com/work-with-me/

5. Are you working against the tide?

There are better times and easier times to do things. Business owners get stressed if they do not do better than last month and last year. What are the results of MOM? YOY? When am I going to hit 6 figures? Multi 6 figures? 7 figures?

Nature works in cycles and we do too. There are times to grow and times to consolidate. The concept of ebb and flow needs to be factored into our businesses, but it's not, we expect always to go full steam ahead. Understanding the cosmic currents helps you understand what the soil is currently fertile for in your life and business.

Knowing what Personal Year you are in helps you actively seek and take the opportunities that are offered to you. Knowing the vibration of the year, the unique experiences, challenges and opportunities of each cycle all add important knowledge and coping skills to your business toolbox, enabling you to work with, instead of against the cosmic current that you are experiencing RIGHT now.

More exciting information to come in Part 3 of this book.

CHAPTER 25

WHAT DO YOU DO IF YOU DO NOT FEEL LIKE YOUR LIFE PATH NUMBER?

By this stage in this book, you will have ascertained that Your Life Path number is THE single most important number in numerology. It is created from using the numbers in your date of birth which it is impossible to change - so it stays with you for your entire life.

What happens if ... you found out your Life Path number AND ....

It didn't resonate. It really did not feel like you at all ...

So you discounted and ignored it, but are seeing other people getting results by understanding their numeric energies.

So, what can you do?

The most important place to start is to confirm that you are a certain Life Path number - so double check using my free Bizology® Life Path app Life Path App - https://josoley.com/life-path-app/

The next step is to look at the day of the month that you are born on. This number is very easy to be. This number comes very naturally, it is the number that we start our life working in, it is the number we are as children and it is the number that is very easy to pick up in someone's energy.

A lot of people stay operating from this number and do not actually engage with their Life Path number. I go into more depth about the day of the month you are born on, in Chapter 32.

Remember, 75% of what is going on is related to your Life Path number

Your Life Path number is what you are destined to do here on earth. In business this is the path to take that makes the most difference. This is where we get all of our results, this is where the juice is, and the real magic happens.

Understanding your Life Path number really helps you connect to what is possible for you and your business.

So how can you connect deeper to your Life Path number?

In my Bizology® sessions with my clients I show them their Life Path number, by connecting them to ...

The Symbology of the Number

I was born on the 4th of the 4th, 4 is about foundations. Remember the story about 4 - we have 4 fingers, 4 seasons, 4 directions etc, in life 4 keeps us organised.

Connecting you to the symbology of the numbers, the stories that your numbers want to tell you and appreciating how you use the number in life, helps you connect deeper to the number.

I also show you other 'abstract information' about your Life Path number, looking at related chakras, colours, crystals, Tarot cards - as all these tools help you connect deeper to your number. We ascertain where you are 'on the spectrum' of the number, by looking at certain keywords and discussing how they resonate.

Characteristics and Goals of the Life Path number in Business

I connect you to how your Life Path number can be optimised in your business and what to be mindful of. We look at the prime interests of the number, the motivation and vibrations of the number, knowing this is useful as you can sense, check and monitor if you are working with these energies and appreciate your ultimate goal and long-term plan.

Lessons of the Life Path number

We are all here to learn. Each Life Path number comes with its own set of lessons. There are certain times of your life when these lessons will play out stronger than others, understanding these lessons help us work with our number instead of against it.

Challenges and Potential Negatives of the Life Path number

As I have said a few times now ☺ (making sure that you are taking notice) we are the negatives of our numbers, anything else is just guidance. When we understand the negatives of our numbers we can stop 'doing' these and pull them up like weeds in a garden and then the positives naturally grow.

Direction of the Life Path number in Business

This is where we look at the potential of your Life Path number, the direction you can ultimately go in to determine what is possible. This is where I bring everything together and show you what is possible for your Life Path number in business. If you have a number, you have it for a reason, so we need to make sure that you use it and not lose it.

Using your Life Path number in business

Using your Life Path number in business is work in progress. It takes time for certain pieces of information to land, to percolate and filter through. Some details may resonate more than others, so this is what you remember as this is what you are here to learn and implement first. I receive messages from my clients months, even years after their Bizology® sessions to say they have listened again and pieces of information have suddenly clicked. We can only learn what we are ready to learn at any given moment.

Compatibility

When you have an understanding of the Life Path number and how it plays out in business, last but not least, I show you the compatibility of the numbers, you can also have compatibility and conflict within your own numbers.

Your Deeper Numeric Chart

We are not just one number - The Life Path number, we are made up of a tapestry of numbers and this is where the real you lies.

Harmony and conflict exist through your numeric chart.

There are numbers that are easy to be.

There are numbers that you are working towards in life, that you are aspiring to and aligning to.

There are numbers that you were in a previous life.

There are numbers where your power lies.

PART 3

USING COSMIC CURRENTS IN BUSINESS

CHAPTER 26

FORGET INTERNATIONAL WOMEN'S DAY - IT'S INTERNATIONAL WOMEN'S MILLENNIUM

At the start of this book, I explained that on 8th March 2017, International Women's Day, I was introduced to a modality that changed my life, my business direction, how I view and relate to myself and others forever.

I attended an event and listened to Richard Abbot talk about Numerology, his opening gambit was ... 'Forget International Women's Day, it's International Women's Millennium!'

Why?

As we are now in the noughties, the 2000s, in the energy of the 2.

In numeric terms 2 is all about the divine feminine, sacred knowledge and using our intuition.

This is the energy we are now all working under as we are living under the umbrella of the 2.

If 2 was a chakra it would be the sacral chakra which is associated with the emotional body, sensuality and femininity.

If 2 was a colour it would be orange.

If 2 was a Tarot card it would be the High Priestess which is all about intuition, mysticism and the subconscious mind.

If 2 was an element it would be water, and water is unpredictable and hard to contain.

If a person is working with the energy of the Life Path 2, it is about being feminine and gentle, 2 energy is not about being forceful. Life Path 2s can feel in flux and be undecided. Life Path 2s deeply feel the need to create balance. Life Path 2s are invested in harmony, sometimes having a foot in both camps as they can see both sides of the story. Life Path 2s are intuitive, having a natural knowing for 'stuff'.

So how does this relate to the 2000s?

The times that we are in now are very feminine in energy, we are in constant change and can be undecided. Now more than ever there is the need to create balance, to see both sides of the story. We can feel that we are going back over old ground, and there is no certainty. These times are also ripe for us to develop our intuition, our physic development, our natural 'knowing' for 'stuff'. Hence the concept that more people are currently 'waking up'.

Remembering that we are the negatives of our numbers, so the challenge for the energy of 2 is that it is sensitive with a capital S, in all senses of the word, and taken to the extreme can be unpredictable, fearful, indecisive, too emotional and invested in safety.

We can see all the above playing out in the millennium that we now live in.

So how can we navigate the 2000s?

One of the ways to understand what is happening now is to compare the energy of the number 2 (2000s) to the energy of the number 1=1900 =1+9+0+0= 19=10=1.

Remember, you are not the number next to you. 1 is definitely not 2 and 2 is definitely not 1.

1 is masculine in energy, it is not a soft vibration. 1 wants to get straight to the point, is very direct, it takes action. It is results led, it wants to go from A to Z. 1 is about independence, innovation and speed.

Living through the 1900s = 1+9+0+0=10=1, we had questions and answers. Men led and women followed, no judgement here that is how it was. We had Reagan, Thatcher and Scargill. Things happened with more certainty and more masculinity. The way we were schooled and parented was more masculine in energy (we had a slipper hanging in my headmaster's office - imagine that now!) That was the vibration of the 1900s and if you were alive in those times you can relate to that.

Now we are in the energy of the 2, there is no certainty and in our lifetime there won't be. We will not live into the 3000s! In order to feel our way forward and navigate these times and to work positively in the energy of 2, we need to cooperate, it is important that we sense the rhythm of situations, develop our sensitivity and interact with the natural flow of life. We need to develop patience and to cultivate the ability to harmonise and work with others.

2 energy in action

To witness the energy of the '2' in the 2000s in action, look at the number of women that run their own businesses, many more than 40 or even 20 years ago. Look again at the more holistic nature of these businesses. Look at the transition of women now playing masculine sports such as Football and Rugby. Look at the more 'inclusive' way we adopt everything we do, be it parenting, schooling, running our businesses, our approach to mental health, the LGBT community and recently the menopause. On the flip side of this people can be super-sensitive, you can't say anything without it being 'un-pc', the 'cancel culture' is a relatively new concept under the energy of the 2, however it is a real thing.

This is a huge concept to introduce you to in a couple of paragraphs, to accept that EVERYTHING will now be different just because years start with a '2' instead of a '1', so this information is literally 'top line', but goes some way to explain why it is not just 'International Women's Day but International Women's Millennium'.

CHAPTER 27

WE WORK IN 9-YEAR CYCLES AND THERE ARE BETTER YEARS AND EASIER YEARS TO DO THINGS

The Personal Year that you are currently in helps you understand what the soil is fertile for right NOW In your life and business.

The operative phrase here is – 'there are better times and easier times to do things'. Sometimes the soil is not fertile for our plans, appreciating what the soil is fertile for can help you move forward in your business.

Important … Personal Years start on your birthday, and they end on your birthday, (they do not run from January to December as some numerology resources can inform you). Personal Years indicate the energy of what you are currently working on in your business. Knowing which Personal Year you are currently in helps you work with the vibration of the year and its energies instead of against it.

The Personal Years run from Personal Year 1 year through to Personal Year 9, we can also experience a Personal Year 11 and a Personal Year 22 within this timeframe. As these are master numbers, we do not reduce them to 2 or 4.

When we enter a Personal Year 1, it is like a brand-new phase of our life for the next 9 years. Forget a new page, or a chapter, or even a new book, it is like a whole new library to explore and discover and we want to treat it as such.

Reality check - we can't bat 100 every single day, it is important to acknowledge this, appreciating that we need ebb and flow and growth and consolidation in our businesses.

Nature is cyclical – so why wouldn't we operate in cycles too? There is a time to plant the seed and a time to harvest it. We too can follow natural cycles to restore our business to natural rhythms. Like nature, we grow, we consolidate and then we grow and consolidate. It is not feasible to expect record years and months all the time, we require the space for our businesses to expand and then bed down. As the saying goes, 'the day you plant the seed is not the day you eat the fruit.'

Universal year energy is what we experience as a collective

At the time of writing this book we are in 2023 = 2+0+2+3=7. So universally the whole world is working under the energy of 7 = The Seeker, an introspective year. (More on Universal Years in Chapter 31).

Individually we are working through our own Personal Year cycle.

Understanding the Personal Years helps us work from a natural flow state in our business, not pushing or forcing.

We can use the years to …

- Focus on projects.

- Adjust to phases of business.

- Know when to take action = bloom.

- Know when to rest = hibernate.

- Look at most magnetic times for our business activities.

- Direct energy and power more efficiently.

- Appreciate some cycles are more favourable than others for achieving certain goals.

We have themes within the year and understanding the year helps us understand the theme and how to make the energy work. When you know energies are coming you can plan for it.

How it plays out for you, depends on your personal numeric energies, Life Path 1 in a Personal Year 1 = you will be in your element – literally!

Personal Years take a month to kick in and Peak 6 months in.

Every year you get the chance to understand how it feels to be that number.

Knowing which Personal Year, you are in is very powerful, as it means you can work with instead of against the tide in your business. This is all happening anyway, we are literally shining a light on what is going on so we can consciously work with the energy of the Personal Year.

Let's look at how we can use the Cosmic Currents to align your business activity to its innate success!

CHAPTER 28

HOW TO CALCULATE WHICH PERSONAL YEAR YOU ARE CURRENTLY IN

You can work out which Personal Year you are in using my free Personal Year Calculator here ...

https://josoley.com/personal-years-app/

Or use the below calculation ...

DAY +
MONTH +
YEAR OF LAST BIRTHDAY =

(If you have not had a birthday yet in this calendar year use last year)

So as an example, the year I was writing this book:

4 + 4 + 2022 = 2030 = 5
I was in a Personal Year 5.

Into

4 + 4 + 2023 = 2031 = 6
A Personal Year 6.

CHAPTER 29

WHAT YOUR PERSONAL YEAR MEANS FOR YOUR BUSINESS SUCCESS

Going deeper with each Personal Year ...

Are you in a ...

Personal Year 1

This is a year to seed the **NEW** in your business, with an independent attitude – go for it.

Personal Year 11

This is a year for all things **SPIRITUAL** in energy in your business - a time to connect to a higher force (it is 11 not 2 as 11 is a master number and we do not reduce it).

Personal Year 3

This is a year for all things **COMMUNICATION** in your business - share your message.

Personal Year 4/22

This is a year for all things **STRUCTURE** in your business – get your ducks in a row.

Sometimes you can be in a Personal Year 22 not a Personal Year 4 (as 22 is a master number and we don't reduce it), this is a year for huge **TRANSFORMATION** in your business that will impact others.

Personal Year 5

This is a year for all things **CHANGE**, expansion and growth in your business - take those opportunities.

Personal Year 6

This is a year for all things **RELATIONSHIPS** and responsibility in your business - work in your community.

Personal Year 7

This is a year for all things **LEARNING** and introspection in your business - get researching.

Personal Year 8

This is a year for all things **SUCCESS** and goal setting in business - set high standards.

Personal Year 9

This is a year to **LET GO** of everything that does not serve so you have space to seed the new in a Personal Year 1.

Then the cycle starts again.

Going deeper ...

Personal Year 1 -
This is a year to start the NEW in your business

- The last year has been about releasing and letting go in your business. A Personal Year 1 is the first year of a new 9-year cycle.

- A time to have a fresh start in business, a year to start all things new, a rebirth year. A year to think ahead, look to the future and be purposeful about what you want to achieve.

- The new things you start this year will seed over the next 9 years. Not everything you seed will grow and that is OK, as the more you seed, the more can grow.

- In a Personal Year 1, new directions and opportunities will be offered and should be investigated and action taken where appropriate.

- Remember YOU are your brand – own what you do. A Personal Year 1 is a year to be innovative, independent and individual, like a Life Path 1.

Personal Year 11 -
This is a year for all things SPIRITUAL in your business

This is a Personal Year 11 not 2 as we are in the 2000s so it gives us an extra digit in the calculation making it a master number and whenever we encounter a master number in numerology, we do not reduce it.

- If you are in a Personal Year 11, you are working with master number energy this year. This is a HUGE year in your life BUT it can be a very emotional year, a turbulent year, so make sure that you have a direction and a plan this year in your business.

- This is a year where you can delve deeper with your spiritual and cosmic connection in terms of meditation and the inner world using these messages in your business.

- You need to implement much more self-care in a Personal Year 11, look after yourself.

- Feelings can change sharply this year, be careful not to overreact and maintain perspective.

- Make sure you are inspired so that you can then inspire others like a Life Path 11.

Personal Year 3 -
This is a year for all things COMMUNICATION
in your business

- After a Personal Year 11 this year's energy is lighter and brighter.

- What you have planted in a Personal Year 1 will start to grow, from seeds to shoots.

- The energy of a Personal Year 3 is about happiness and joy and there is an element of good luck (which you don't want to push).

- 3 is 'The Communicator', so it is the year to put your written and spoken words into the world, a creative year in your business.

- A year to put yourself out there, meet and greet people in your business community. Enjoy yourself but watch your business expenses as 3s like to spend money.

- It is a year to be enthusiastic, imaginative and optimistic like a Life Path 3.

Personal Year 4 -
This is a year for all things STRUCTURE in your business

- After the lighter energy of the Personal Year 3, a Personal Year 4 is about structure, control routine and systems.

- It is a practical period, a time to make plans and build stronger and secure business foundations. Bring in new structures and systems, get those business ducks in a row for future growth.

- A year to write a list of everything you need to do in your business and work through it step-by-step. Not a year to rush things in business - nothing happens quickly.

- The Universe will shine a light on weak areas in your business, so this is a year to mend the cracks to reconstruct your life and business.

- A Personal Year 4 is a year to be hard-working, organised and practical. Patience, attention to detail and common sense is required like a Life Path 4.

Personal Year 5 -
This is a year for all things expansion, growth and CHANGE in your business

- After the slower pace of last year, a Personal Year 5 is a year to take off again in your business, but in a different direction from the last 4 years.

- Change is in the air for your business - growth, expansion and adventure is the optimal energy for this year.

- A Personal Year 5 is THE year that new business opportunities are available to you. There will be travel opportunities and chances to take your business into new areas and expand your horizons.

- Watch out for 'Shiny New Object Syndrome!' Ensure you take action to make the opportunities happen and do not become too impatient or scatter your energies.

- Shake the business bag and try new things. It is a year to remain adaptable and flexible like a Life Path 5.

Personal Year 6 -
This is a year for all things RELATIONSHIPS and responsibility in your business

- A year where all things 6 play out - relationships, love and family. To move the business forward concentrate your efforts on relationship marketing, audience building and serving your tribe.

- This is a year of service; in business you will take on more responsibility than usual but be careful not to bite off more than you can chew.

- Community is the buzzword, a year to celebrate and connect with others. It's self-employment, not 'by-your-self' employment in a Personal Year 6.

- Reassess the business relationships in your life. Relationships can either flourish OR breakdown this year, they go either way.

- Be careful not to over give this year and watch those boundaries. It is a year to be loving, caring and kind like a Life Path 6.

Personal Year 7 -
This is a year for all things LEARNING and research in business

- This is a quieter year. A year to look inwards – an introspection and self-reflection year.

- This year you will be called to reflect, refocus and replenish so spending time alone will be required. Modern life doesn't really support a Personal Year 7, it is THE year to have a sabbatical.

- Opportunities will come your way if you are prepared to wait. You can make money but not always on your time scale. Do not push too hard for success and wealth – that is next year.

- This year is a good pre-launch phase - read, learn, study, think, analyse. Spend time on the research and development of your products and services.

- It is a year to be a seeker, thoughtful and introspective like a Life Path 7.

Personal Year 8 -

This is a year for all things SUCCESS and wealth and goal setting in business

- This is the ultimate year of abundance and achievement in the 9-year cycle. A year to harvest.

- However, success and material achievement take place relative to what you have sown over the last 7 years. Remember, nothing comes from nothing. Karma can ALSO be at play with regards to what you have sown, you can strike it rich OR lose it all, depending on your behaviour in the last 7 years.

- The focus in a Personal year 8 is on goal setting, action and results, a year for higher ticket products and services, quality over quantity.

- You will face more responsibilities during the year, promotions, business ventures and the ability to achieve.

- It is a year to be professional and have high standards like a Life Path 8.

Personal Year 9 -

This is a year to LET GO of everything that does not serve so you can kick start your business again in a Personal Year 1

- A Personal Year 9 is a year to purge, shed, delete and release in your business.

- A time to tie up all loose ends from the last 9 years, letting go of what has held you back, business relations that are no longer working, processes and systems that need to go, zero inbox etc!

- A year of endings, out with the old this year and in with the new next year. Be careful not to start anything too new in your Personal Year 9 as when you get into your Personal Year 1 it can feel old and you may not be interested anymore.

- Think of yourself as a Caterpillar in your chrysalis metamorphosing into a Butterfly.

- A Personal Year 9 is a time to be compassionate, giving and caring but you will also need strong boundaries like a Life Path 9.

Personal Year 22 -
THE WORLD IS YOUR OYSTER YEAR I have not seen anyone have this year for over 10 years, as the calculation is ending in 4 not 22, not everyone experiences a Personal Year 22.

- A Personal Year 22 is a year to reach for the stars, it is a year to remember.

- Some people never experience a Personal Year 22, so if you do, then go for it - anything is possible.

- You have the ability to 'go beyond' this year, limitations are lifted - go after your goals.

- Your energy and mental ability will be at an all-time high, so make sure you ground what you do and have a sense of reality.

- What you do this year will help all - a time to be 'An Architect of Change' = Life Path 22.

CHAPTER 30

WHAT IT MEANS FOR YOUR BUSINESS CHANGING PERSONAL YEARS

When we change Personal Years, we experience a transitioning process.

I offer a complimentary discovery call to my ideal clients who are Bizology® Curious and want to know more about how Bizology® can help them in their business RIGHT NOW.

You can book yours here - https://calendly.com/Bizologywithjosoley/20min?month=2023-04)

RIGHT NOW, is in capital letters, as at the beginning of the call, I ask them to give me their date of birth and full name and whilst I am crunching key numbers, I ask them to provide me with a 'stream of consciousness' about what is going on for them in their life and business **RIGHT NOW**, their goals, their wins, their challenges, go for it, tell me all.

Very early into the call, through this 'stream of consciousness' I am able to identify if they are in a Personal Year where the soil is fertile for growth or consolidation. If they are struggling, they will be trying to push a cart up a hill instead of relaxing into the energy of the year. If the tide is out, they can feel confused and I witness this in their demeanour and language.

When you are aware of your Personal Year it gives you permission to work with the energy of the year instead of against it.

If you have been in a 'Go, Go, Go' year and everything is flowing and the emphasis is on growth (for example a Personal Year 8), and then you hit a year that the Universe wants you to release, shed and let go (for example a Personal Year 9) then this can feel confusing, you may ask yourself 'What have I done wrong, why are things suddenly not working?' It is not that you have done anything wrong, or that it is not working, there are different themes in your business that you need to be focusing on **RIGHT NOW**.

Take the Personal Year 4 for example, 4 is about foundations, so in a Personal Year 4 you will want to get your ducks in a row, to support your doing this the Universe will shine a light on anything that is weak in structure so that you can fix it, in order to create structure in your business. A Personal Year 4 is not a light and optimistic year, where you can put your word into the world, that is a Personal Year 3. It is also not an adventure, change and expansion year where you have opportunity at every turn that is a Personal Year 5.

You are not the number next to you also applies to Personal Years in your business.

A lot of my clients reach the end of their Personal Year 3, having had a great time and spent lots of money on life and business expenses, as Life Path 3s like to spend money (every year you get the chance to feel what it's like to be that number), and say to me, I really feel the need for systems and operational structure in my business. SYSTEMS = Save Yourself Time, Energy and Money. YES! you feel the energy coming in, these cosmic currents are happening anyway regardless, we are just shining a conscious light on it.

The 9-year cycle is needed and welcomed and if we can work with it instead of against it, it creates game changing results in our business.

Some of the years, like the Personal Year 4 can feel heavy, nothing happens quickly and the emphasis is on dotting the i's and crossing the t's. When you go into your Personal Year 5 and the focus is on freedom and movement, you can find it difficult to shift gears. If 4 were an element it would be earth and if 5 were an element it would be spirit - these two elements are very different in energy so the transition between the 2 years can take time to embed.

As you head towards your birthday and your next Personal Year is incoming, if you haven't actioned what you need to do within the vibration of the year, the Universe will ramp up the energy of the year, so that you do.

This is where I come in, it is my job to show you which Personal Year you are in and ensure you are 'working within the energy' of the year in your business so that you deliberately work in alignment with the Personal 9-Year cycle, teaching you ways to work in your business if the tide is not in for growth.

If you feel that you are spinning your business wheels, and nothing is really happening compared to previous years, there is a reason. If you feel your business is taking off exponentially, the energy of your Personal Year will be supporting this (including the work you are doing in your business in the years leading up to this).

One of the main realisations I have come to throughout my journey with Numerology, developing Bizology® and in particular, working with the Cosmic Currents is this ... 'If the cake is not ready, you do not want to take it out of the oven.' The modern world has us running from the assumption that we can do anything at any time, however, this is not true, as sometimes we are not ready for things to come into fruition.

Timing is always paramount, knowing this information is where your power lies in business.

CHAPTER 31

UNIVERSAL YEARS IN BUSINESS

As we work in Personal Years we also work in Universal Years.

Why did the sky fall down in 2020?

At the beginning of 2020 I wrote a blog, 'A Bizology® Viewpoint - What 2020 is really asking of us?'

The essence of the blog was to give a 'heads up' of the huge energy that was coming, 2020 = 2+0+2+0 = 22. In numerology, 0 represents God, so we gently move it out of the way, leaving us with 22. 22 is a master number, which means that there are HUGE forces at play. To work with the energy of 2020, we needed to use the energy of 4, 2+0+2+0 = 4. 4 being about structure, we required this energy to navigate 2020. When I carry out Bizology® sessions with my Life Path 22 clients, we don't want them to work in 4, we want them to activate their 22'ness, however as 22 is such a massive energy, globally we needed support to navigate 2022.

We can safely say that 2020 was a powerful year, an unprecedented year, energetically it was a Karmic year. The 20th Major Arcana card in the Tarot is Judgement, so 2020 = double judgement, one judgement is enough! The side effects and the fall out of 2020 will last for a long time, and as we are experiencing a few years later, a clean-up operation is still taking place both logistically and emotionally.

My comments about using the energy of 4 in 2020 were ... (an extract from the blog) ...

'If your foundations are not solid in a master number 22 year, there is more chance of wobbling. More structure, less chance of

wobbling. The more structure you have with your foundations this year the less problems you will have. We are being called to get our foundations sorted. We need firm foundations to move forward in a Universal 22 year.'

Then I wrote a blog 'A Bizology® Viewpoint - What will 2021 mean for your business?'

2+0+2+1 = 5. 5 is about change, freedom, growth and expansion.

The 5th major Arcana card in the Tarot = The Hierophant. This card is about Teaching, Spiritual Advancement, Unity, looking at the details of everyday life, sanctuary of community, education, studying in groups etc.

The Hierophant (also called The Pope) balances the energies between above and below and offers spiritual counsel, it also represents the nature of our own faith and the quest for oneness.

After 2020 many people did (and some were forced to) look at themselves, their lives and businesses. The 5 / Hierophant energy in 2021 assisted and shone a light on spiritual advancement, asking what were the next steps for you? This was not separated from your business growth but an integral part of it.

Then we headed into 2022 = 2+0+2+2 = 6 = The Nurturer, and yes you guessed it I wrote a blog - 'A Bizology® Viewpoint - What will 2022 mean for your business?'

6 is all about relationships and responsibility. In the Tarot the 6th Major Arcana card is 'The Lovers' – which is about love, intuition and duality but also about choices. Representing an opportunity to move on, choosing what you want with a commitment to yourself.

2022 was no doubt a Universal Year where all things 6 played out – community, groups, love and family. Our business relationships played a pivotal role this year and it was easier to take on more responsibility than usual, so we had to be careful not to take on more than we could handle. In order to move our businesses forward the focus was on relationship marketing, audience building and serving your tribe.

2022 - What was also very important is the 22 in 2022, not as potent as 2020 – but we still had the 22 master number in the year 2022. 22 can be the equivalent to 5000 volts and with any master number we need a plan. 2022 had a nod to 22, and wherever we have 22 we have a STRONG energy.

22 combined with the 6, gave us the choice to reconnect with our relationships with ourselves and others, giving us the ability to create change and transformation within these areas, which was critical when the world around us was very uncertain.

What will 2023 mean for your business?

2+0+2+3 = 7 = The Seeker. 2023 is a 7 Universal Year.

The 7th Major Arcana card in the Tarot is The Chariot – this card is about will power, progress, personal strength, action, determination and moving forward.

The Charioteer (in 2023 = YOU) will need good inner stillness. Inner determination and focus will be required in business this year, if you have a good 'inner connection', then the energy of the Chariot can be used.

What helps with having a good 'inner connection'? Introspection and personal growth. Seek to know yourself more. Have faith in yourself and do not give up or try to take shortcuts in business. We can overcome any obstacle if we have faith in ourselves. Alongside this achievement personal effort will be required.

A key word for 7 is introspection, in 2023 you will be called to do some inner searching. If life gets too busy it will feel confusing. Take time to think things through, get some rest, take time out to create balance and then act.

It was evident that as we entered 2023, no one visibly hit the deck running with all guns blazing, it has been a slower burn Universal year under the energy of the 7.

The rest of the decades of the 2000s

2024 $2+0+2+4 = 8 =$

A Universal 8 Year - A year for high standards and professionalism.

2025 $2+0+2+5 = 9 =$

A Universal 9 Year - A year for service and compassion.

2026 $2+0+2+6 = 10 = 1 =$

A Universal 1 Year - A year for new beginnings and independence.

2027 $2+0+2+7 = 11 =$

A Universal 11 Year - A year for inspiration and Spirituality.

2028 $2+0+2+8 = 12 = 3 =$

A Universal 3 Year - A year for communication and creativity.

2029 $2+0+2+9 = 13 = 4 =$

A Universal 4 Year - A year to work hard by implementing structure, routine and systems.

CHAPTER 31

Decades

Alongside this, pay attention to the decades that we experience.

The 60s - was about peace and love and the Beatles - and 6 is about love.

The 70s - was about Gen X and fashion - and 7 is about being unique.

The 80s - was about Yuppies, Dallas and shoulder pads - and 8 is about money and success.

The 90s - was about the credit crunch and 9 is about shedding and endings.

We are currently in the 2 decade - a feminine decade, amplifying the 2 energy - remember - 'It's not International Women's Day it's International Women's Millennium.'

PART 4

YOUR BIZOLOGY® COMPASS

CHAPTER 32

YOUR APPROACH NUMBER - UNDERSTANDING THE DAY OF THE MONTH YOU ARE BORN ON

There are 7.9 billion (ish) people on the planet, we don't divide everyone into 11 numbers ... this would be as generic as saying I am Aries and you are Leo. Like your astrological chart has depths, so does your numeric chart.

Each and every one of us are multi-layered and completely unique. To stand any hope of understanding ourselves and how we operate in our businesses we must break ourselves down, by going deeper with our numeric chart.

Q.   How can you personally navigate your Life Path number to achieve the results you desire in your business?

A.   By using the day of the month that you are born on.

The Approach Number, the day of the month that you are born on, shows how you can uniquely navigate your Life Path number.

I was born on the 4th, so the number I use to navigate my Life Path 1 - The Leader, is the number 4.

4 is all about planning, organisation and detail. A friend once said to me 'It serves you well.' Exactly, there are no mistakes, if you have a number, you have it for a reason. My approach to my Life Path 1, The Leader - an inventor, innovator and independent person, is to plan, be ultra-organised, disciplined and use systems to implement structure in my business.

Using 4, The Builder is an easier path for me to take than 1, The Leader. I am mindful that I do not solely operate from 4 energy, as this is my comfort zone number, and what happens in comfort zones? not much. Stepping up and showing up in my business and using my Life Path 1 to be the lone ranger – self-employed and develop my own practices and methods, not just being a 'me too', but also using the energy of the number 4 to do it my way which is to be organised and in control.

1 = The Leader. 1 is all about being self-employed and bringing something innovative into business - hence the creation of Bizology®.

What is easy to do for me is to be The Builder who Leads. No, I need to be The Leader who Builds - this knowledge alone has been GAME CHANGING for me in my business. That is Bizology® - that is what I do and how I show you how to create massive results in your business.

I am also mindful of the negative of 4, being a workaholic, being too fixated on the plan, being resistant to change. The trick is to be aware of the negatives to use the positives of the 4 so I can navigate and fully own being a Life Path 1 - The Leader. Make sense?

CHAPTER 33

HOW YOU PERSONALLY NAVIGATE YOUR LIFE PATH NUMBER IN BUSINESS

Understanding your deeper numeric chart shows you how YOU can uniquely operate and build your business.

The date of the month you are born on is the number that we use to navigate your Life Path number. This number is called your Approach number, how you are approaching your Life Path number.

This number is actually easier to navigate, and many business owners stay operating from this number, although the trick is to master our Life Path number.

***Caveat - Below I have connected you to some well-known people that are born on the X date of the month. Now this process can alienate you as you may not particularly like or relate to the certain person I mention, and in turn be turned off the number. Please have an open mind, by referencing certain people I am showing you the energy of the number. I have also taken the utmost care to ensure the dates of birth are accurate by checking multiple sources, but we can't be 100% certain that the information available to the public is correct.

Are you born on the 1st of the month?

- You will get noticed in business and have a strong sense of will.

- Self-employment will be of interest as independence is important to you.

- You can become a good leader.

- You will be ambitious and will want to act on this.
- Be careful not to focus solely on your needs in business.

Born on the 1st
Abraham Maslow / Gabby Bernstein / Joanna Lumley

Are you born on the 2nd of the month?

- You will be sensitive to your business environment.
- Use your innate intuition and take the time to develop this.
- Are good at seeing both sides of the business coin.
- Will want to pay attention to the details.
- Can prefer working in partnerships and teams instead of solo endeavours.

Born on the 2nd
Brittney Spears / David Beckham / Mahatma Gandhi

Are you born on the 3rd of the month?

- You will have the ability to communicate in business.
- Use your gift of imagination and creativity.
- There will be the need to speak and connect to people in your business community.
- Will have the ability to build an audience.
- Be careful not to become too scattered and restless with your projects.

Born on the 3rd
Anna Wintour / Gareth Southgate / Greta Thunberg / Martha Stewart

Are you born on the 4th of the month?

- You are not scared of working hard and applying yourself.
- Will want to be organised in your business.
- Likes a plan - loves a list!
- Need to build foundations in your business and have the ability to do this.
- Be careful not to be too stubborn or rigid in your business endeavours.

Born on the 4th
Beyonce / Karren Brady / Maya Angelou / Rosa Parks / Russell Brand / Touker Suleyman

Are you born on the 5th of the month?

- Will have the ability to be versatile and adaptable in business.
- Always on the lookout for the next 'new shiny object' in business.
- Have a love for freedom and travel.
- Opportunity will come knocking at your business door on a regular basis, make sure you act upon this.
- Be careful not to start 20 business tasks and finish none.

Born on the 5th
Adele / Esther Hicks / Walt Disney

Are you born on the 6th of the month?

- Will have a responsible streak.
- You will be drawn to communities and groups.
- Teaching and using your voice in business will appeal.
- A family / people theme will be connected to your business.

- Be careful not to strive for perfection in all that you do - it does not exist!

Born on the 6th
Dalai Lama / Jay Shetty / Mel Robbins / Sigmund Freud

Are you born on the 7th of the month?

- You will want to learn, to gather information and ask questions.
- Specialising in business will work well for you.
- Opportunities will come to you when you least expect them.
- Will need space to think things through.
- Be careful not to procrastinate and overthink in business.

Born on the 7th
Bear Grylls / Eva Peron / Lewis Hamilton / Simon Cowell

Are you born on the 8th of the month?

- The world of business and its many facets will be of interest to you.
- Adopt a professional and executive approach in all that you do.
- Goal setting will be important.
- Will have an ambitious streak in business.
- Be careful not to be too critical of self and others.

Born on the 8th
Sir David Attenborough / Elvis Presley / Louise Hay / Michelle Mone / Pink / Stephen Hawking

Are you born on the 9th of the month?

- You are here to help others in business.

- Adopt a broad minded outlook.
- Will have an artistic and creative streak in business.
- Will have a sensitive and emotional approach when working with others so ...
- Watch those business boundaries.

Born on the 9th
John Lennon / Marie Kondo / Simon Sinek

Are you born on the 10th of the month?

- Equipped with a strong ability to lead others in business.
- Independence is important - you will not like being told what to do.
- Continually develop and innovate your products and services.
- Will have an original and dynamic streak that is there to be used in business.
- An independent character - make sure you let people help you when required and remember it's not always about you.

Born on the 10th
Bono / Holly Willoughby

Are you born on the 11th of the month?

- A master number birthday (see Chapter 6).
- You are here to inspire others in business.
- Your connection to Spirit, Source = God will be important to develop.
- Will need to manage your energy as 11 is an extreme energy.
- Be careful not to overreact.

Born on the 11th
Deborah Meaden / Salvador Dali

Are you born on the 12th of the month?

- Creative energy is there to be used in your business endeavours.
- Gifted at writing and presenting.
- Carry an air of enthusiasm and optimism.
- Will be able to develop the ability to sell in business.
- Watch your expenses - 12/3s like to spend money.

Born on the 12th
Florence Nightingale / Jeff Bezos

Are you born on the 13th of the month?

- Perceived to be lucky for some!
- Will work hard for the things that are important to you.
- Are more sensitive than you first appear.
- Super organised - make sure you do not come across as officious.
- Watch the tendency to be unreasonable.

Born on the 13th
Robbie Williams / Sara Cox / Taylor Swift

Are you born on the 14th of the month?

- You will have a versatile approach to all that you do.
- Managing large endeavours will work well for you.
- International business dealings will be attractive.
- When focused can achieve a lot - 14/5 can go 2 ways - construct or destruct (See Chapter 23).
- Watch your impatience streak.

Born on the 14th
Albert Einstein / Donald Trump / King Charles III / Gary Vee / Mark Zuckerberg

Are you born on the 15th of the month?

- Loyalty will be a non-negotiable for you in business.
- Justice will feature through the work that you do.
- Will learn new things easily in business.
- Your home and family is important, but you will also need free reign in your business.
- Be careful not to 'help' (interfere) with others too much.

Born on the 15th
Ariana Huffington / Claudia Winkleman / Emma Watson / Martin Luther King / Will.i.am

Are you born on the 16th of the month?

- You have a thirst for knowledge and will want to implement this information into your business.
- It will be necessary to step off the online stage from time to time.
- Trust your intuition and never go against your gut.
- You will have a connection with all things mystical.
- Watch the tendency to be too self-absorbed.

Born on the 16th
Davina McCall / Oscar Wilde / Madonna / Rebecca Campbell

Are you born on the 17th of the month?

- Financial matters will be your focus in business.
- You will be honest and straightforward.

- Have the ability to manage large projects.
- Can have a ruthless streak when required.
- Develop the ability to listen to others - they are sometimes right!

Born on the 17th
Ed Sheeran / Michelle Obama / Muhammed Ali

Are you born on the 18th of the month?

- You will have an understanding character.
- Ability to see and connect to the bigger picture in business.
- Will need to adopt an adaptable approach and try things more than once - keep going!
- Can end up as leaders even when not looking to be one.
- Will need to put your foot down in business from time to time.

Born on the 18th
Brene Brown / Brad Pitt / Elizabeth Gilbert / Nelson Mandela / Peter Jones / Richard Branson

Are you born on the 19th of the month?

- You will have a unique, even unconventional approach to business.
- Self-employment will be very attractive to you.
- Will have a tenacious streak in business.
- Do not like being told what to do - but will need to consider the needs of others.
- Watch the tendency to be hyper focused to the detriment of everything else.

Born on the 19th
Coco Chanel / Dolly Parton

Are you born on the 20th of the month?

- Will have a gentle and emotional side.
- Access to a tactful and diplomatic streak that can be used in business.
- Have the ability to carry out very detailed work.
- Working in small teams works for you - TEAM = Together Everyone Achieves More.
- Careful not to be hyper-sensitive at times.

Born on the 20th of the month?
Gary Barlow / Louis Theroux / Rhianna

Are you born on the 21st of the month?

- Will be comfortable being the centre of attention.
- Use your communication skills in business - speaking, podcast, masterclasses, courses, teaching.
- Under the lucky 3 - ensure not to fritter away these opportunities.
- Have a lot of energy, be conscious to use this wisely by ...
- Developing the ability to concentrate and focus in business.

Born on the 21st
Kim Kardashian / Paloma Faith / Prince William / Queen Elizabeth II / Usain Bolt

Are you born on the 22nd of the month?

- Born on a master number day - a powerful day of the month. (See Chapter 6)
- You have the ability to accomplish a lot in business.
- Trust your instincts and first impressions.

- Will be drawn to worldly causes you can help through your business.
- Can be very highly strung and will need strategies to manage this strong energy.

Born on the 22nd
Ant Middleton / Deepak Chopra / Meryl Streep

Are you born on the 23rd of the month?

- You will seek excitement in business.
- Are quick witted and energetic, others will find you charismatic and charming.
- The NEW appeals in business - and you will like to make decisions quickly.
- Can take calculated risks.
- Watch your impulsive tendencies as these can get you into trouble.

Born on the 23rd
Carrie Green / Mo Farrah / Sara Davies / William Shakespeare / Zoe Ball

Are you born on the 24th of the month?

- A trustworthy, loyal and responsible attitude.
- Can achieve a lot in business if you manage your energy, actualise your ideas and put plans into place to make them happen.
- Will have a creative and artistic streak to use in business.
- Home is an important place for you.
- Watch over-dramatising things in business.

Born on the 24th
Lord Alan Sugar / Jennifer Lopez / Lionel Messi / Mary Berry / Steve Jobs

Are you born on the 25th of the month?

- Can have a secretive side - a part of you that you do not show to the world.
- Have the ability to create original solutions to business problems.
- Don't ignore your strong intuitive insights.
- Making decisions can take a while.
- Careful not to hoard - especially paper and information.

Born on the 25th
Alicia Keys / Elton John / Pablo Picasso

Are you born on the 26th of the month?

- Have an executive ability that can be used.
- Education will be important to you - continue to train in your business subjects.
- Good with helping others manage their money - watch your own affairs too!
- Make sure you keep a balance between home life and business life.
- Can appear aloof to others, even though this is not your intention.

Born on the 26th
Mother Teressa / Steven Bartlett / Stormzy

Are you born on the 27th of the month?

- Will have a humanitarian streak and be able to understand the feelings of others.
- Have a determined but calm manner with all business dealings.
- Will learn to work well with others throughout your business journey.
- Selecting the correct business will be important.
- Remember no is a full sentence.

Born on the 27th
Derren Brown / Jamie Oliver / Wolfgang Mozart

Are you born on the 28th of the month?

- Leadership and self-employment will call you ...
- Although your success will need support.
- An independent and determined streak will be evident - although you are more sensitive than you first appear.
- Have strong will - but do have the ability to work well with others.
- In search of freedom make sure that you do not over catastrophize situations.

Born on the 28th
Alex Polizzi / Bill Gates / Elon Musk / Kylie Minogue / Lady Gaga / Mary Portas

Are you born on the 29th of the month?

- Working with a master number energy = 2+9 = 11, see Chapter 6.

- Will find yourself in situations where you inspire others in business.
- Developing and maintaining a connection to Spirit will be important.
- Ensure you have clear plans with all your business endeavours.
- Life can be dramatic at times - ground and manage your emotions!

Born on the 29th
Oprah Winfrey / Michael Jackson / Tony Robbins

Are you born on the 30th of the month?

- Will have a very strong ability to communicate as are strong conversationalists.
- Born entertainers in business, as love being at the centre of attention.
- Have lots of energy to put into creative projects, watch you do not get bored.
- Will need free reign for your business endeavours.
- Watch your tendency to exaggerate - you will have a lot to say!

Born on the 30th
Sir Winston Churchill / Warren Buffet / Vincent Van Gogh

Are you born on the 31st of the month?

- A strong character in business, who will face tests in life.
- An unusual ability to be practical and creative - a potent mix!
- Will not be afraid of working hard in business.

- Will achieve more if you have solid foundations in place.
- Watch being argumentative for the sake of it.

Born on the 31st

JK Rowling / Steph McGovern

PART 5

BIZOLOGY® IN REAL LIFE

CHAPTER 34

WELL-KNOWN PEOPLE IN NUMBERS

This is an interesting but important exercise; in this part of the book I show you 'well-known' people who are working with specific Life Path numbers. Connecting the number to people that we know in 'real life' helps us see how the different aspects of the numbers play out, both in the positive and the negative. Light bulbs moments happen here as you can see the Life Path numbers working out in real time.

***Caveat** - Below I have connected you to some well-known people that are born on the X date of the month. Now this process can alienate you as you may not particularly like or relate to the certain person I mention, and in turn be turned off the number. Please have an open mind, by referencing certain people I am showing you the energy of the number. I have also taken the utmost care to ensure the dates of birth are accurate by checking multiple sources, but we can't be 100% certain that the information available to the public is correct.

Life Path 1 = The Leader	Walt Disney

Summary Biography

Walt Disney, born on 5th December 1901 in Chicago, USA. He was a creator, a Motion Picture and Television producer and Showman. As a pioneer of animated cartoon films, Disney created characters including Mickey Mouse and Donald Duck and was the mastermind of Disneyland Amusement Park in California and Disney World in Florida. Disney is now celebrated as one of the world's largest entertainment enterprises.

Working with Life Path 1

Walt Disney was working with the energy of the Life Path 1 - The Leader. 1s are innovative powerhouses, they have more ideas than any other number. I don't think you could get more innovative than creating a cartoon mouse and turning it into a 55+ billion US dollar empire!

Walt Disney got the inspiration for Mickey Mouse from a tame mouse at his desk at Laugh-O-Gram Studio in Kansas City, Missouri. *'They used to fight for little pieces of cheese in my wastebasket when I worked alone late at night. I lifted them out and kept them in wire cages on my desk. I grew particularly fond of one brown mouse. He was a timid little guy. By tapping him on the nose with my pencil, I trained him to run inside a black circle I drew on my drawing board. When I left Kansas City to try my luck at Hollywood, I hated to leave him behind. So, I carefully carried him to a backyard, making sure it was a nice neighbourhood, and the tame little fellow scampered to freedom.'*

Walt Disney was born on the 5th, so the way he approached his Life Path 1 - The Leader was to use the energy of 5, imagination and resourcefulness to bring his creations to life. Freedom to birth his artistry in his own way would have been vital.

Quoting Walt Disney ...

"I only hope we never lose sight of one thing - that it all started with a mouse". - Walt Disney

Other well-known people working with Life Path 1 ...

Anna Wintour / Ariana Huffington / Deborah Meaden / Florence Nightingale / Lady Gaga / Lionel Messi / Martin Luther King / Maya Angelou / Sara Cox / Steve Jobs / Steven Bartlett / Stormzy

Life Path 2 = The Sensitive   Michelle Obama

Summary Biography

Michelle LaVaughn Robinson Obama, born on 17th January 1964, is an American attorney and author. She served as First Lady of the United States from 2009 to 2017 as the wife of former President Barack Obama, the first African American woman to serve in this position.

Working with Life Path 2

Michelle Obama is working with the energy of the Life Path 2 - The Sensitive. The strength of the Life Path 2 gives Michelle the perceptive and intuitive ability to be aware of others in the world. Using these gifts in the role she is here to play in life gives her the innate ability to see both sides of the story, to create harmonious outcomes and balanced environments.

Born on the 17th, Michelle uses the energy of 8 to approach her Life Path 2, giving her a talent for business, a good sense of financial acumen and sound judgement in executing what she undertakes.

Quoting Michelle Obama ...
"When they go low, we go high" - Michelle Obama

Other well-known people working with Life Path 2 ...

David Beckham / Derren Brown / Gabby Bernstein / Gareth Southgate / Gary Vee / Jenifer Lopez / King Charles III / Madonna / Rosa Parks / Tony Robbins / Wolfgang Mozart

Life Path 3 = The Communicator   Alan Sugar

Summary Biography

Lord Alan Michael Sugar, born on 24th March 1947, is a British business magnate, media personality, author, politician and political adviser. In 1968, he started consumer electronics company Amstrad, which became his largest business venture; in 2007 he sold his remaining interest in the company for £125m.

Sugar was the chairman and part-owner of Tottenham Hotspur from 1991 to 2001, selling his remaining stake in the club in 2007 for £25m. He is also known for being the big boss for the BBC reality competition series 'The Apprentice', broadcast since 2005. According to the Sunday Times Rich List, Sugar became a billionaire in 2015.

Working with Life Path 3

Lord Alan Sugar is working with the energy of the Life Path 3 - The Communicator. Life Path 3s are blessed with the gift of the gab and are here to use this gift. I heard Lord Sugar say that he is actually quite funny on the Apprentice but most of it ends up on the cutting room floor as they want to portray the big bad business mogul wolf! Life Path 3s are born salespeople, need intellectual stimulation, are witty and have many business ideas.

Born on the 24th, Lord Sugar uses the energy of 6 to approach being a Life Path 3. 6s are great in business as they understand how people feel, so they are good at creating solutions to problems which is ultimately what business is. He also has a 9 in his chart, so the 3 / 6 / 9 energy gives him access to a higher business consciousness.

Quoting Lord Sugar ...

"If you enjoy what you do, don't be afraid of expressing your enthusiasm. Enjoyment is infectious." - Lord Sugar

Other well-known people working with Life Path 3 ...

Ed Sheeran / Esther Hicks / Gary Barlow / Kylie Minogue / Rebecca Campbell / Rhianna / Salvador Dali / Simon Sinek / Touker Suleyman

Life Path 4 - The Builder   Marcus Rashford

Summary Biography

Marcus Rashford MBE, born on 31st October 1997, is an English professional footballer who (at the time of writing) plays as a forward for Premier League club Manchester United and the England national team. Rashford's England debut was in May 2016 when he became the youngest English player to score in his first senior international match. He has also represented England at the 2018 and 2022 FIFA World Cup.

Marcus is also a campaigner against racism, homelessness and child hunger, using his platform to be a political activist and philanthropist to drive societal change. He has received widespread praise and recognition for his efforts.

Working with Life Path 4

Marcus Rashford is working with the energy of the Life Path 4. Life Path 4s are conscientious and not adverse to hard graft. Discipline and focus are the keys to Marcus's success. Life Path 4s can have a serious and rigid side to them, using structure they apply practical methods to lay solid foundations.

Born on the 31st, gives Marcus another 4 - mirroring the above and adding strength of character, he will not be scared of applying himself and working hard to get the job done. With double 4 he will need to watch being too serious and obsessive about detail.

Quoting Marcus Rashford ...
"For me, sometimes it's more important to perform well in training and know that I am improving rather than scoring in a game. It's doing the hard work, day in, day out." - Marcus Rashford

Other well-known people working with Life Path 4 ...

I do not know of any as most well-known people are working with the energy of Life Path 22. 4s are worker bees.

Life Path 5 - The Adventurer   Mark Zuckerberg

Summary Biography

Mark Elliot Zuckerberg, born on 14th May 1984 is an American business magnate, internet entrepreneur, and philanthropist. He is known for co-founding the social media website Facebook and its parent company Meta Platforms (formerly Facebook, Inc.), of which he is the chairman, chief executive officer, and controlling shareholder.

Zuckerberg attended Harvard University, where he launched 'a version' of Facebook in February 2004 with his roommates. Originally launched to select college campuses, the site expanded rapidly beyond colleges, reaching one billion users by 2012. Zuckerberg took the company public in May 2012 with majority shares. In 2007, at the age of 23, he became the world's youngest self-made billionaire. In 2010, Time magazine named Zuckerberg among the 100 most influential people in the world. In December 2016, Zuckerberg was ranked tenth on Forbes list of The World's Most Powerful People.

Working with Life Path 5

Mark Zuckerberg is working with the energy of the Life Path 5 - The Adventurer. He will need the freedom to execute his large-scale entrepreneurial endeavours. 5s can have several projects on the go at once, exploring new opportunities and new horizons. Variety is the spice of business.

Born on the 14th - gives Mark another 5, a quick and analytical mind, he will be headstrong and want his own way. Resilient, finding solutions to most problems. Life Path 5s can roll the dice in business, so with double 5s Mark will have the courage to take risks in business.

Quoting Mark Zuckerberg ...

"The biggest risk is not taking any risk". - Mark Zuckerberg

Other well-known people working with Life Path 5 ...

Abraham Maslow / Beyonce / Brene Brown / Elizabeth Gilbert / Eva Peron / JK Rowling / Marie Kondo / Russell Brand / Simon Cowell / Vincent Van Gough

Life Path 6 - The Nurturer   Karren Brady

Summary Biography

Karren Rita Brady, Baroness Brady, CBE, born on 4 April 1969, is a British business executive and television personality. Former managing director of Birmingham City F.C., Vice-chairman of West Ham United F.C., and an aide to Lord Alan Sugar on The Apprentice. She is a Conservative member of the House of Lords and has been a Small Business Ambassador to the UK Government.

Brady is a regular writer for national newspapers and magazines and has also published four books including two novels. Her most recent book, 'Strong Woman' aimed at inspiring women in business, was a Sunday Times Bestseller.

Working with Life Path 6

Karren Brady is working with the energy of the Life Path 6 - The Nurturer. Life Path 6 is based on the energy of family, so running a football club is very 6 in energy as it is about community and collaboration. 6s are great in business as they are keen observers of human nature. As consumers, we don't buy our way into something, we buy our way out of something, we want our problems solved and a Life Path 6 understands this.

Karren is born on the 4th, so will use the energy of 4 to be conscientious and disciplined. She will create secure foundations in business through implementing plans and systems to drive herself and others forward.

Quoting Karren Brady ...

"Good managers ensure good outcomes, but great leaders can deliver a vision by getting people to work together." - Karren Brady

Other well-known people working with Life Path 6 ...

Albert Einstein / Brittney Spears / Jeff Bezos / John Lennon / Louis Theroux / Meryl Streep / Michael Jackson / Warren Buffet / Zoe Ball

---

Life Path 7 - The Seeker   **Queen Elizabeth II**

Summary Bio

Queen Elizabeth II, born on 21st April 1926, in London, England.

From 1952-2022, Queen Elizabeth II was the Queen of the United Kingdom, Canada, Australia and New Zealand, also Head of the Commonwealth and the Queen of 12 independent countries, including Jamaica, Barbados, Bahamas, and Papua New Guinea.

The Queen ruled for 70 years, longer than any other Monarch in British history, becoming a much loved and respected figure across the globe. Her extraordinary reign saw her travel more widely than any other monarch, undertaking many historic overseas visits. Known for her sense of duty and her devotion to a life of service, she was an important figurehead for the UK and the Commonwealth during times of enormous social change.

The Queen saw public and voluntary service as one of the most important elements of her work. Having links as Royal Patron or President with over 600 charities, military associations, professional bodies and public service organisations.

Working with Life Path 7

Queen Elizabeth II was working with the energy of the Life Path 7 - The Seeker. 7s have fine minds, are analytical thinkers, capable of great concentration and theoretical insight and deliver creative and practical solutions to problems.

7s demand much of themselves and set high standards. They need solitude and time and space to contemplate their ideas. Aware of the need to 'come off stage', I always say, you can't rush a 7 and you couldn't rush the Queen, she needed to take the time to come to her own decisions.

Born on the 21st, her approach to her Life Path 7 was 3, to communicate with her people.

Quoting Queen Elizabeth II ...
"Some cultures believe a long life brings wisdom. I'd like to think so. Perhaps, part of that wisdom is to recognize some of life's baffling paradoxes such as the way human beings have a huge propensity for good, and yet a capacity for evil."

Queen Elizabeth II

Other well-known people working with Life Path 7 ...

Bear Grylls / Deepak Chopra / Elon Musk / Muhammed Ali / Peter Jones / Pink / Sir Winston Churchill / Stephen Hawking / Taylor Swift / William Shakespeare

Life Path 8 - The CEO   Nelson Mandela

Summary Bio

Nelson Mandela, born on 18th July 1918, in Umtata, South Africa. Mandela was a South African anti-apartheid revolutionary, politician, and philanthropist, who served as President of South Africa from 1994 to 1999, and was the country's first black chief executive and the first elected in a democratic election.

Mandela served 27 years in prison. Amid growing domestic and international pressure and fears of racial civil war, President F. W. de Klerk released him in 1990. Mandela and de Klerk led efforts to negotiate an end to apartheid, which resulted in the 1994 multiracial general election in which Mandela led the ANC to victory and became president.

Mandela was a controversial figure for much of his life. Although critics on the right denounced him as a communist terrorist and those on the far left deemed him too eager to negotiate and reconcile with apartheid's supporters, he gained international acclaim for his activism. Globally regarded as an icon of democracy and social justice, he received more than 250 honours, including the Nobel Peace Prize. He is held in deep respect within South Africa, where he is often referred to by his Thembu clan name, Madiba, and described as the 'Father of the Nation.'

Working with Life Path 8

Nelson Mandela was working with the energy of the Life Path 8 - The CEO. 8s are gifted with natural leadership. They have great talent for management in all walks of life, especially in business and financial matters, where they contribute to the greater vision and purpose. They are naturally attracted to positions of influence and leadership.

Mandela used his 8 energy by inspiring people to join him in his quest, even when they are incapable of seeing what he saw. 8s are good judges of character, which served him well in attracting the right people and directing them along the lines of his vision.

Born on the 18th, he would have used the energy of 9 to approach his Life Path 8, broad-minded, idealistic, and compassionate. 9 understands life is of service to society. Nelson had a greater social role to play that required a blend of the practical and the humanitarian. Having a keen sense of what would work (Life Path 8), but at the same time directed those efforts toward some greater good (18/9).

Quoting Nelson Mandela ...

"I learned that courage was not the absence of fear, but the triumph over it. The brave man is not he who does not feel afraid, but he who conquers that fear." - Nelson Mandela

Other well-known people working with Life Path 8 ...

Claudia Winkleman / Joanna Lumley / Martha Stewart / Oscar Wilde / Pablo Picasso / Usain Bolt

Life Path 9 - The Humanitarian   Alex Polizzi

Summary Bio

Alessandra Maria Luigia Anna Polizzi di Sorrentino, born on 28 August 1971, known as Alex Polizzi, is an English hotelier, businesswoman, and television personality. Since 2008, she has appeared on The Hotel Inspector on Channel 5.

Born of Italian descent Alex Polizzi comes from a family of hoteliers. Her mother is the Hon. Olga Polizzi, a hotel designer who is a daughter of Lord Forte and the sister of Sir Rocco Forte. Polizzi read English at St Catherine's College, Oxford. She trained at the Mandarin Oriental, Hong Kong, and worked for Marco Pierre White.

Polizzi and a baker boyfriend started a wholesale bakery, Millers Bespoke Bakery, supplying bread to Selfridges, Harvey Nichols and Fortnum & Mason. She managed the Hotel Endsleigh in Milton Abbot, near Tavistock in Devon, which is owned by her mother Olga. In 2021, Polizzi and her mother opened The Star in Alfriston, in East Sussex, in their first joint venture.

Working with Life Path 9

Alex Polizzi is working with the energy of the Life Path 9 - The Humanitarian. She is here to be benevolent by helping others. When I first worked out her Life Path number, I thought she would be a Life Path 1 – The Leader or a Life Path 8 – The CEO due to her business acumen and no-nonsense approach to helping failing hoteliers turn their hotels into reputable businesses.

Born on the 28th, the number she uses to approach her Life Path 9 is 1 = The Leader, which is evident through her innovative and entrepreneurial approach to business.

Upon further investigation Alex has more 9s in her chart, she is very passionate about helping hoteliers, so we see her 'service over success' task of 9 kick in. 9 is the strongest single number in existence and it has the biggest job to do. Life Path 9s are here to help others.

Quoting Alex Polizzi ...
"But now, more than ever, I think people really want to be looked after – and we really want to look after people." - Alex Polizzi

Other well-known people working with Life Path 9 ...

Adele / Alicia Keys / Carrie Green / Elvis Presley / Greta Thunberg / Jamie Oliver / Louise Hay / Mahatma Gandhi / Mary Berry / Michelle Mone / Mother Teresa / Robbie Williams

Life Path 11 - The Spiritual Teacher   Steph McGovern

Summary Bio

Stephanie Rose McGovern, born on 31st May 1982, originally from Middlesbrough began her career with the BBC network first working on Tomorrow's World. She studied Science Communication and Policy at University College London. At the age of 19, she was awarded the 'Young Engineer of Britain' after saving Black & Decker £150,000 a year by improving production techniques used for the Leaf Hog product.

Steph McGovern has presented BBC Breakfast show, BBC Radio 5 Live's Wake Up to Money and On the Money and presented Pocket Money Pitch for CBBC. She has co-presented the consumer series 'Shop Well for Less' for BBC 1. Steph also joined the BBC's Watchdog presenting team and co-presented 'Can Britain Have a Pay Rise?' for BBC Two and has been both a panellist and host on 'Have I Got News for You.'

The COVID-19 pandemic meant that she began presenting 'The Steph Show' from her front room in March 2020. The show eventually launched in September 2020 as 'Steph's Packed Lunch.'

Working with Life Path 11

Steph McGovern is working with the energy of the Life Path 11 - The Spiritual Teacher. Working with a master number Steph has the ability to see more, be more and do more. Wanting to do much for humanity, she will be quick paced, have great intellect and can take things up a level. This is the positive of the 11 energy, a steeliness, a drive, coupled with the ability to inspire. Steph will need to watch her energy and keep her feet on the ground as 11 is a strong master number influence.

Born on the 31st, to approach her Life Path 11 master number, Steph will use the energy of 4. Her impetus will be economical, conscientious, honest and loyal. Helping others save money, her passion for delivering the truth and ensuring everything she does has merit.

Quoting Steph McGovern ...

"Business leaders regularly complain that young people don't leave school with the right skills. Encouraging young people to be entrepreneurs makes the connection between school and the world of work, teaching them about practical thinking, teamwork, communication and financial literacy." - Steph McGovern

Other well-known people working with Life Path 11 ...

Coco Channel / Emma Watson / Mo Farrah / Paloma Faith / Prince William

Life Path 22	Richard Branson

Summary Bio

Sir Richard Charles Nicholas Branson born on 18th July 1950, is a British entrepreneur, investor, commercial astronaut and business magnate. In the 1970s he founded the Virgin Group, which today controls more than 400 companies in various fields.

In March 2000, Branson was knighted at Buckingham Palace for 'services to entrepreneurship.' For his work in retail, music and transport (with interests in land, air, sea and space travel), his taste for adventure and for his humanitarian work, he has become a prominent global figure. In 2007, he was placed in the Time 100 Most Influential People in the World list.

Working with Life Path 22

Richard Branson is working with the energy of the Life Path 22 - The Architect of Change, possessing great potential for success. 22s have the ability to effectively bring together the necessary elements - people, ideas and resources - to realise their goals. Life Path 22s can make an enduring impact on the world as they naturally understand large corporations and have the ability to think and act on an international scale.

As a visionary Richard is gifted with the ability to see the potential in a given idea, but also the practical methods that will bring it to fruition. He understands intuitively the limitations of ideas - what will work and what will not.

Born on the 9th, the way that he approaches his Life Path 22 is by having a strong commitment to his ideals and vision.

Quoting Richard Branson ...
"A business is simply an idea to make other people's lives better."
- Richard Branson

Other well-known people working with Life Path 22 ...

Ant Middleton / Bill Gates / Bono / Brad Pitt / Dalai Lama / Davina McCall / Dolly Parton / Donald Trump / Elton John / Holly Willoughby / Jay Shetty / Lewis Hamilton / Kim Kardashian / Mary Portas / Mel Robbins / Oprah Winfrey / Richard Branson / Sara Davies / Sigmund Freud / Sir David Attenborough / Will.i.am

CHAPTER 35

CONVERSATIONS WITH JO - KNOWING YOUR NUMBERS - REAL LIFE STORIES

The 3 below interviews are with real life clients of mine that I interviewed on the Bizology® Soundbites Podcast. I have been given permission by each to publish the interview, and all details were correct at the time of recording - March - July 2022.

Knowing Your numbers - Real Life Stories with Hanieh Vidmar

Hanieh Vidmar started her health career in a pharmacy as a Health Advisor and then a Dispensing Technician, today she is a Health Coach and Phlebotomist for The Wellmacy. Hanieh is an advocate for having regular blood tests as a fantastic way to stay on top of your health, she is currently studying to be a Nutritionist so that she can help people make key changes in their lives to be healthier and live better.

Jo – "Tell me about your career and business journey to this point ..."

Hanieh - "When I was studying towards my A levels I worked in a pharmacy, I studied media at university because I really wanted to be a TV presenter or a Movie Director, I absolutely loved watching the makings of movies and how they put this music video together.

When I graduated, I started working in television. Towards the end of my time at university, a TV presenter visited and afterwards I bombarded her asking her about the TV industry. She gave me a job on her show, which was on an African channel on Sky TV where I did live TV presenting and absolutely loved it. I worked with an incredible woman, who gave me an amazing opportunity and met so many people plus I got the opportunity to work at the BBC. TV is a very competitive industry and it was very challenging, however, I also took the initiative and launched my own YouTube channel interviewing celebrities.

Fast forward a few years and I got a job recruiting. I loved helping people find work and when they were placed in the job, asking them 'Are you happy?' 'Is this what you want to do?' 'Is this your thing?' I really enjoyed the people aspect. I've tried so many different things, I opened a salon with my sister, Mummy blogging, Public Speaking. In the last seven years I've tried everything but nothing stuck.

During lockdown I went for a blood test, and I thought to myself, 'I can do that.' So I booked a course and qualified as a Phlebotomist. I was fascinated by the science of why we should take blood. My sister had opened a beauty clinic in central London, I enquired if I could do blood tests at the clinic, and was told I could provide the Phlebotomy services but to interpret the results, I needed to be a nutritional therapist or a doctor.

I decided to become a nutritional therapist and signed up for a college course in London. I'm now in my second year. I can't wait to fully utilise this knowledge by bringing blood testing and nutrition together. I have been on a personal journey since my days at the pharmacy and I feel I have finally found my thing".

Jo – "Hanieh is working with the Life Path 6. The Nurturer, all about love, family, relationships and taking responsibility for others. What made you want to learn more about your numeric energies in business?"

Hanieh – "I heard you on Janet Murray's podcast and what you were sharing really spoke to me. I booked a session to learn more, and was blown away by the things that you shared about my numbers. It helped me understand myself on a whole new level, embracing my positives and working on my weaker areas. Bizology® has helped me to manage and better deal with my challenges in life and after our sessions I feel more equipped to navigate them".

"I am a nurturer; I do look after people; I love taking care and going the extra mile for people. I've always been that person, you helped me not only understand that is an inherent part of me, but embrace it, because that is who I am".

Jo – "6 is about caring. It is about community and service, how has learning more about your Life Path 6 helped you in business?"

Hanieh – "I am very much invested in my family and communities. I like being kind to people and helping my clients. I always think that when I'm older I will be that grandmother who looks after everyone. That's the legacy I'd like to leave behind and where I can, I will.

Since working with you I have practised implementing stronger boundaries and appreciate that it's OK to say no and to look after myself a bit more. I'm not very good at confrontation, so I will happily say, 'No problem, I can do that', when sometimes I should say 'Unfortunately, I can't right now.' That has been my biggest Aha moment, that it's OK to put me first, even as a Life Path 6."

Jo – "If a family is in crisis, a 6 can feel in crisis, a Life Path 6 can give and give to others. When I ask a Life Path 6 - 'How are you?' They will tell me how everyone else is apart from them. What about them? How are they? Has that helped, appreciating some of the pitfalls and downfalls and things to watch out for as a Life Path 6?"

Hanieh - "Definitely. To stop feeling guilty if I do spend some time by myself. In the Bizology® Magic Circle you show us that there are better days and months to spend time by yourself. I've started to do that guilt free."

Jo – "That is huge for a Life Path 6".

Hanieh – "I know! I will go to a gallery by myself and enjoy 'me' time. Instead of thinking 'OMG, I should be doing this, this and this ... who is going to pick up my son etc ...' I am relied on a lot by my family, the business, the clinic and my clients. Putting myself first at times has helped me reconnect to myself.

You have helped me accept that it's perfectly fine for me to pull myself away for a couple of hours every now and then. I enjoy these pockets of time on my own and prescribe them to myself, they are good for me."

Jo – "Other Life Path numbers will not appreciate how monumental it is for a Life Path 6 to do that, it is massive!

Even though you are a Life Path 6, we all operate in 9-year cycles. You are currently in a Personal Year 7. Like the phrase at '6s and 7s' you are not the number next to you. The Personal Year 7 is about introspection. It's not a busy year, even though you are a busy Mummy, it's a year to learn, a year to study, a year to research. You have worked with me for a few years now, you were in a Personal Year 5 when we first met, a year for change. Then you went into your Personal Year 6 as a Life Path 6, so you would have felt in your element - literally. Now you are in your Personal Year 7. How has understanding the years and appreciating that you need ebb and flow and growth and consolidation in your business helped you?"

Hanieh – "When I was in my late teens / early 20s I would experience certain situations and think, that was a slow month, or that was a good month for work or that was a good month for travel etc. However, you never think about numerology or cycles, you just think that was just the kind of month I had.

By understanding the cosmic cycles and my Personal Years and the information you share through your work and in your membership - 'The Bizology® Magic Circle' I appreciate the energy of the cosmic influences. I know I'm in a Personal Year 7 and has been and is a slower more introspective year for me. I feel it, I can feel the slowness, the steadiness, the desire that I have to learn. I am learning something every day, whether it's for an exam, research for an assignment or a personal project. I have learnt so much this year, and it's not something I would have consciously done before. Everything I'm doing this year is setting me up for the next 20+ years ahead with a new business that I am fully committing to.

If I didn't know that I was in a Personal Year 7, I would be so frustrated, not understanding why everything was slower. I would be thinking, 'Why isn't this happening?' 'Why am I not getting XYZ NOW?' Things are happening, the results come in, it's just slower paced.

When you know this information, you can use it to your benefit and remember that there is no need to stress, everything is happening when it's meant to. I've started to embrace the slowness, it's no big deal, everything's happening in its own time, whenever the time is right. I don't need to be frustrated when things don't happen immediately."

Jo – "People expect to bat 100 all the time and you can't. You live in London, one of the biggest and busiest cities in the world, it never sleeps. However, like nature, we need growth and consolidation, yin and the yang energy.

What would you say to somebody if they were Bizology® curious?"

Hanieh – "I think if you are looking for a way to catapult yourself forward, to get organised but more importantly to understand yourself on a much deeper level, then definitely use numerology, specifically Bizology®. If you Google numerology loads of websites, come up, it's Bizology® that is the difference. The way you do things, the way you help people run their business and get organised in line with their numeric energies and Personal Years. The process you use takes away a lot of guesswork. 'Why is this happening? Because you're in a Personal Year XYZ' 'What should I post on social media this week? You help us create our posts according to the energies of the week.

If you want to understand yourself as a business owner, if you want to get more organised and have a plan of action to move forward in your business then Bizology® is a game changer. It's really helped me better understand myself, other people and the happenings in my life. It's helped me create a business plan and goal set and when something doesn't go to plan (as that's life) you can appreciate why. It's a unique, fun way of seeing and doing business. Some people might use a diary or a planner to run their business, for me, Bizology® has been a great tool.

If you are Bizology® curious, speak to Jo, you have been brilliant for me, and all the other women in the membership. When we talk to each other and meet up, everyone's just so excited to be there. Using numerology in business might sound 'woo woo' but honestly, it's brilliant. It makes sense. So don't be Bizology® curious, definitely speak to Jo."

Jo – "Thank you very much. One of the words you keep using is organised. I was born on the 4th of the 4th, and 4 is about being organised. Hanieh was born on the 31st of July. The same as JK Rowling, the 31st is a very powerful day - 3+1 = 4. Your approach is the same as me, 4 which is why you like to feel organised. You like to have a plan; you apply

yourself; you're not scared of hard work. You are loyal, you are reliable. Some of the strengths of being born on the 31st is observant, strong character and conversationalist – which we can see in this interview you are."

Hanieh – "Also born on the 31st is Primo Levi – an Italian chemist, Milton Friedman a Nobel Prize winning economist, Wesley Snipes - the American Actor and George Baxter a 19th century painter."

Jo – "I love the fact you know that! 'Is there anything else you'd like to share before we wrap up?"

Hanieh – "Having sessions with you helps you fall into your skin, and you stop fighting yourself. Everyone loves to talk about themselves, although sometimes compliments are hard to receive. When I have sessions with you, and you share things about my numbers, it's nice to acknowledge the things that I can develop, as well as working on the negatives of my numbers as you connect me to these as well.

In the Bizology® Magic Circle you also share the energy of each day and the things that we can expect and implement. I think you have a great service; you are very organised as shown in your numbers and the way you do things. I've absolutely loved working with you and love being in your presence.

So just keep going, and I hope more people will come into your world and see for themselves how amazing Bizology® is and what it empowers you to do."

Jo – Thank you

You can find Hanieh here ...
Instagram - @haniehvidmar and
www.haniehvidmar.co.uk

Knowing your numbers - Real Life Stories with Samantha Littlejohn

Samantha is a Clinical Hypnotherapist and Happiness Coach. The creator of 'The Habits of Happiness Programme', which has been delivered through Scotland, in schools, Youth Sector, corporate and through her private coaching business.

She is passionate about helping women to uncover their habitual patterns that have been keeping them in cycles of stress, overwhelm and self-sabotaging behaviour, to break free and create the life they truly desire, through her simple seven step coaching process.

Samantha has also recently launched her seasonal subscription box - 'Membership Retreat in A Box', which is so much more than a box full of goodies. It is designed to give you the tools and techniques to help you build new self-care routines, overcome stress and anxiety and improve your overall well-being. It brings everything you need for a holistic wellbeing retreat right to your door.

Jo – "Hi Samantha – thank you for joining me to share about how you learnt more about yourself through your numeric energies, is there anything you would like to add to your introduction?"

Samantha – "Hi, I'm Samantha, I am passionate about helping individuals master their habits for success and happiness in every aspect of life and business. After experiencing burnout, I discovered the power of positive emotions and habits and started teaching others. Today, my vision has grown into 'The Habits of Happiness Coaching', and I have also pivoted my business to help other female business owners avoid the dreaded burnout. Having been there myself, I know the signs and have made it my mission to give these superwomen the tools and strategies to create balance in their life and business. Saying goodbye to guilt and excuses, I'm here to help them put themselves at the centre of their life and business."

Jo – "That's important and so needed. It's key at this stage to explain that Samantha is working with the energy of the Life Path 8 – The CEO. The CEO is all about high standards and goal setting in business. Life Path 8s nail it in business, they intuitively know what to do. What made you want to learn more about Bizology …?"

Samantha – "I first heard you speak in a group for coaches led by Karen Ramsay-Smith, 'Radiant Leaders' now called 'Super Vision', and I was just amazed at how much my Life Path number resonated. I booked your package and during the sessions you explained about my numeric energies but also about my business energies, its name, the date I set it up, and how the numbers of my business can have an influence on its success. I loved learning more because not only was it fascinating, but it also made so much sense."

Jo – "75% of what's going on in your life is related to your Life Path 8, The CEO. The 8th Major Arcana card in the Tarot is the Strength card. The image on the card is a picture of a woman holding a lion, she is engaging with the lion, she is wearing a crown and she is ruling. Using this energy in business relates to empowering people to rise. How did appreciating being a Life Path 8 help you in your business?"

Samantha – "The biggest Aha was that I realised I had been avoiding the energy of Life Path 8. I was not embodying the 8 – The CEO, since understanding this I have put my energy into working on my business, expanding it, laying foundations and working on my strengths to really embrace The CEO, and show up in my life and my business using this energy. To be honest, I was working more in the energy of 1 – The Leader."

Jo – "Fantastic, great to hear that you are working more in Life Path 8 – The CEO, this is where the business magic will happen for you and this is what Bizology® is about. You mention 1, you are born on the 28th = 10 = 1, so it's easy for you to hang out in the energy of 1 = The Leader. You have had businesses in the past that were very solo, independent businesses. It's easy for you to work in leadership energy, but it's important for you to step into the energy of 8 = The CEO, because that's where the results happen. That is the path you are here to walk this lifetime. How have you embodied your Life Path 8 in your business?"

Samantha – "That has where the shift has been, that was the piece that spoke to me, that I was drawn to. Deep down I knew that I needed to shift gears from being a solo-entrepreneur into a more executive role. My vision is massive, the change that I want to make in the world is huge, but I can't do that on my own. I needed to step up, take responsibility and drive the business forward. Since our sessions that has been my focus, the decisions I'm making now are related to making that a reality. Embracing my numbers has helped me embody this shift, creating a Limited company and making 'Habits of Happiness' a social venture. I now have a company board, we are receiving funding, running bigger programs, and I am acting and being The CEO of the company. It's allowed me to give myself permission to step into this new version of me. Also, identifying some of my weaker areas has allowed me to hire people to work alongside me in the business in these areas, which has been important."

Jo – "Do what you do best and outsource the rest! Fantastic, being born on the 28th = 10 = 1 The Leader, it's easy for you to be the Leader who has 8 skills and dabbles as The CEO = 1/8, but we want you to be The CEO who leads = 8/1."

Samantha – "This knowledge has helped me recognise that

this is where my true strengths lie to fully step into the role of The CEO. I've been an entrepreneur since I was 23, every time I started a business on my own, I knew I was meant to be doing it in a more professional way, I now understand this energetically and am working towards making it a reality."

Jo – "There are 7.9 billion (ish) people in the world. We don't just divide everybody into 11 numbers, it goes deeper than that. We look at 5 key numbers in your chart, your name and your business energies. There are numbers that are easy for you to be, which for you is the energy of 1, there are numbers we want to work towards and there are numbers that can trip you up.

We also look at your cosmic currents as we work in 9-Year cycles. When we were working together, you were finishing your Personal Year 9, which is about endings, you are currently in your Personal Year 1, all about seeding the new for the next 9 years. How has understanding your Personal Years helped you navigate your business right NOW?"

Samantha – "It made a lot of sense; my business partner is also in the same Personal Year as me. When we were in our Personal Year 9, this allowed us to let go of that which no longer served the business. We were aware that we were focusing on the small details, we stopped doing that and focused on the business vision. When we got into our Personal Year 1, we received so much clarity on the direction that we wanted to take the business in. It's been amazing to have that awareness because it helps you to focus on strategy, planning and the key direction to take the business in. So rather than trying to fight it or feel that you're questioning it, you can trust that the energy is leading you in the right direction."

Jo – "Nature doesn't get stressed out, she blooms, she

sheds, she hibernates and we need to do this too. I love that you said not to focus too small, 9 is about vision. You currently have 2 months left of your Personal Year 1, it is important to consciously, intentionally and deliberately squeeze every last drop of this year, we don't want to waste any of the Personal Year 1 as it's fabulous energy to seed the new. What new energy have you seeded this year?"

Samantha – "There has been a lot, I have set up a new limited company. I have also launched a new service, 'My retreat In A box' helping you nurture yourself in business from the inside out. I used to be a Holistic Therapist, but self-care is a lot more than having the occasional treatment. I wanted to be able to support people as they came out of the pandemic by helping them navigate the crazy times we are in. By allowing women (it's predominantly aimed at women) to prioritise themselves, building self-care into your life as a woman is super important.

Whether you have a family, a business, a career, a partner or are single, as women we push ourselves to the bottom of our to-do lists. It's important to remind ourselves that we must implement boundaries, as that's what it all boils down to. That is what I am passionate about, helping women by providing them with the self-care tools they need to take care of themselves. All the products and services they need access to are online, coaching is available, and they also have support from me."

Jo – "It sounds like a brilliant resource, also great to seed a new product in your Personal Year 1 that will grow over the next 9 years, and you started a new Limited company under the umbrella of the Personal Year 1. Any new faces, new places or new spaces?"

Samantha - "I have met new faces; I've hired new people who are working in the business, and I am working with 5 new contracts.

This Personal Year 1 has also allowed me to think about the new things that I wanted to start in my life, the new things I wanted to seed and grow within. Starting new yoga practices, new breathing techniques and reminding myself to practice the things I teach."

Jo – "I wanted to ask about your plans for your Personal Year 11. You still have a couple of months of your Personal Year 1, but a Personal Year 11 is intense as 11 is emotional. It is also a year to be inspired and inspire other people. In a Personal Year 11 it is important to look after your energy. Do you have any plans for next year?"

Samantha – "My plans are to expand and to teach other people the 'Habits of Happiness' by licensing, training the trainer to spread my teachings and the authenticity of the message. My Personal Year 1 has been about getting more clarity on the new things that the business needs, it's given me a lot of clarity around the next steps. Expanding the business the way that is optimum, making sure I also look after my energy."

Jo – "I've loved hearing all your wins and how you have stepped into your Life Path 8 and made the most of your Personal Years. What would you say to someone if they were Bizology® curious? If they are thinking about it but they are sitting on the fence?"

Samantha – "Bizology® has really changed and shifted the way that I looked at my business. The sessions were very in-depth, you helped me create a plan for each month related to my personal cosmic currents. Understanding my numeric energies helped me move forward in business, creating such a shift, you get so much out of the sessions. I would say to anyone - go for it."

You can find Samantha here ...

Since this interview Samantha stepped fully into her Personal Year 11 and shifted her retreat in box to 'The Take Time Out Membership' to align with her true message of building self-care into becoming an important habit not just a one-off treat.

Explore - The Take Time Out Membership here ...

https://retreatinabox.kyvio.net/take-time-out/

You can connect with Samantha at ...

Facebook: @jane.sam.12914

Instagram:@samanthajanecoaching

plus:@thehabitsofhappiness

Website: https://www.thehabitsofhappinesscoaching.com

Knowing Your Numbers - Real Life Stories with Marie Fraser

Marie known as The Boundary Queen, is a certified coach, clinical hypnotherapist and integrative therapist with a wealth of experience and knowledge on how to create happy and successful relationships.

Daily we are involved in a myriad of relationships from daughter, sister, lover, mother, partner, friend, co-worker, leader, client, entrepreneur. The success and happiness of every single relationship is dependent on letting them know how we want to be treated and what behaviour is and more importantly is not acceptable to us.

Marie's mission is to help ambitious, professional women create happy and successful relationships by setting, communicating and maintaining their personal and professional boundaries so they can confidently say "NO" and take control of their lives without feeling guilty. When you say 'Yes' to everyone else - you are saying no to yourself.

Weak and inconsistent boundaries create indecision, overwhelm, a lack of self-trust and self-confidence. Relationships flounder, making life miserable and hard, causing stress and anxiety, which if left unaddressed, can lead to depression and burnout.

Jo - "I'm really excited to talk to you about all things Marie Frazer and all things boundaries. Marie is working with the energy of the Life Path 6, 6 is all about relationships, responsibility, connection, and community. About impact over income. What do we need when we're serving others? Boundaries. What does Marie help people manage and navigate? Boundaries. There are no mistakes, if you've got a number, you've got it for a reason. Before we go deeper, please can you share a little bit more about you?"

Marie - "I basically help people who are not living their truth, they are saying yes to things they don't want to say yes to. They might be too afraid to say no, for all sorts of reasons. Primarily my clients are women, I think that as girls, when we are growing up, we're taught to share, not to be selfish, etc, and that's all very well and good, but what we aren't taught is not to overstretch ourselves. We can end up giving too much of ourselves and our energy, putting everybody else first and then we are at the bottom of the pile losing all sense of ourselves.

This patterning and behaviour can stem from childhood or later life experiences when maybe we are afraid to say no because we don't want to lose the partner, the client, the job. When you are living in fear you are not living your truth, for some people that can be for a considerable number of years, as they lead such unhappy lives for so long that they then become riddled with resentment and anger. Those negative energies have such a detrimental impact on our health and wellbeing, and manifest in stress, anxiety, even depression and burnout.

I'm not advocating for everyone to say no to everything, being selfish just doing what you want when you want. I'm saying respect yourself, and when you respect yourself, you get the respect of other people. We need to show people how we want to be treated. It's about living your truth and voicing how you feel."

Jo – "We definitely teach people how to treat us. I love the fact that boundaries are your niche. No is a full sentence, it's very important that we give from the overflow of the cup, and not the cup itself. What made you want to learn more about your numeric energies?"

Marie – "I met you at an event that you were speaking at, and whilst I'd heard of numerology, I knew absolutely nothing about it. I was intrigued by your Bizology® presentation, and it got my juices going to find out more."

Jo – "Marie is working with the Life Path 6, 6 is the only number who understands how people feel. I follow you on LinkedIn, your posts are fabulous, great imagery and motivational quotes, but reading deeper you really nail it with regards to the boundaries piece. What was the biggest Aha moment knowing that you are a Life Path 6, through your Bizology® sessions?"

Marie – "Appreciating on a deeper level, that Life Path 6, The Nurturer was all about relationships and family, that was spot on. For me, it's important that people can lead a happy and successful life. I believe that should be the case for everybody, not just people that I love.

The biggest realisation was related to where I should put my energies in business. You explained that in business Life Path 6 works well one-to-many, rather than 1-2-1. I am an introvert and my energy can become very depleted when I'm surrounded by lots of people and distractions, so it was something that I'd never even considered. It opened my eyes to new potential markets and I have started to put together group programs, that was a real Aha moment.

During that session I said, 'Can I really do group programs with the work I do?' Now I can see how obvious it is. My cup is full when I see people being happy and being successful. So why not do that for lots of people at the same time, rather than just 121."

Jo – "My energy is very 121 because I'm a Life Path 1. 6 is about groups, tribes, family, communities. Being a Life Path 6 doesn't mean you can't work 121, of course not, however, with the energy of 6 wherever there's a network, an event, teams - that energy will really help you flourish, develop and move forward. That's where the growth lies for Life Path 6s in business.

You are born on the 2nd, 2 is The Sensitive, you mentioned being an introvert, this is also related to the energy of the 2. The day of the month we are born on is easier for us to be. It's easy for you to work in the energy of the 2 = The Sensitive, emotional and intuitive. The real magic happens in the energy of the Life Path 6. So instead of being The Sensitive who sometimes nurtures we want you to be The Nurturer who's sensitive. How did that feel when I showed you those numbers and how they play out, one is easier to be, but one is where the results lie?"

Marie – "It all made sense, one of the things that stood out was that it was almost like a yin and a yang that I was opposing rather than accepting. Since I have embraced the group and tribe element of my 6, I feel much more grounded and I feel that is my mission and my path to work in this way."

Jo – "You are a loving mum, and really close to your sons,

and that was playing out in your personal life, but now you are bringing that energy into your business."

Marie – "It was revolutionary, such a strong word, but it's true."

Jo – "Nothing is too strong when it comes to knowing your numbers. It gives yourself permission to be yourself in business."

Marie – "I'm very much of a 'What you see is what you get kind of gal', although in business, I want to come across as in control, as professional. My job is to help people and sometimes they are in very difficult circumstances, the nurturing part of me has always been there from a very young child. Justice and authenticity are very deep values of mine. I don't think there was anything you shared that felt out there, on a deeper level it made a lot of sense to me. Working with you confirmed and consolidated that yes, I am doing what I should be doing that I am definitely on the right path."

Jo – "Life Path 6 is all about integrity, about ethics, about justice. I had a look at your website, and I couldn't see any client reviews or testimonials. I asked you why they were not on your website? When you gave me the answer, I thought that is very Life Path 6. So, tell me why you don't have any reviews or testimonials on your website?"

Marie – "The reason I don't have testimonials on my website is because it's against my professional ethics. With the Advertising Standards Authority, you've got to be able to back things up, people could write absolutely anything. Let's face it, nobody's going to put a bad review on their website. I just feel they are very sweeping and not to be trusted. I think that personal recommendation is much more valid than a testimonial that could be neither the truth or a fabrication of the truth."

Jo – "That was a big realisation for me about Life Path 6. I

always learn so much about the numbers in action when I do the Bizology® sessions. That is Life Path 6 working in integrity, so thank you for working in your Life Path 6.

One of the main pieces of work we do together through the Bizology® sessions is showing you which Personal Year you are in. When we started working together you were in a Personal Year 5, which is all about change, opportunity and growth. How did it feel when I showed you that you had just come out of your Personal Year 4 (a slower year) and were now in your Personal Year 5?"

Marie – "It made so much sense, I have started to widen my network, which has been a big source of change and expansion for me. As an introvert, (I'm not shy or anything), it's about being conscious where I put my energy. I think I had been a little lazy, maybe related to just coming out of lockdown, so I decided to get out there and meet new faces and go to new places. As a result of going to in-person events I've met some interesting new people. I've also learnt new things. I've increased my visibility both on social media, and through networking. I've also put myself forward to speak at various events, which is not something I would have normally done. I'm embracing this year of change and stepping up. It's not a case of going outside of my comfort zone, it's more about consciously taking new opportunities rather than consciously not!

With regards to the tribe element of the Life Path 6, working one-to-many, rather than 1-2-1, I've looked at changing the way that I work incorporating group sessions and group programs. I'm really excited to be embracing this, I sensed and saw that I need to flip and change this year, which has brought about a new season, new things, new opportunities, and new horizons which I definitely feel ready for."

Jo - "The key phrase, the key essence, the key energy of the Personal Year 5 is opportunity. Every year we get the chance to feel what it's like to be another number. So, in a Personal Year 5 it's about taking advantage of opportunities.

What would you say to somebody if they were Bizology® curious, as it's a fascinating subject, and it might be quite nice to know your numbers, but what does it really mean?"

Marie – "Every single one of us can get into a state of 'stuckness.' Thinking 'Am I on the right path?', 'Am I doing the right thing?', 'Should I be doing something else?'. We can all suffer from bright shiny object syndrome, spread ourselves too thin or go down rabbit holes. If you feel you are at that stage or in that state, then I would say speak with Jo about your numbers as you can see where there might be a disconnect somewhere and get clarity on how to move forward.'"

You can find Marie here ...

www.mariefraser.com

Instagram: @boundarymanagementqueen

Linkedin: https://www.linkedin.com/in/marietfraser/

PART 6

WORDS ARE SPELLS · THAT'S WHY WE CALL IT SPELLING!

CHAPTER 36

YOUR NAME IS NOT WHO YOU ARE - IT IS WHO YOU LOOK LIKE YOU ARE

You can't change your date of birth, it is impossible, so your key numeric energies never change. However, you can change your name and when you change your name you change your life, as the letters of your name are related to numbers which hold a vibration.

Read that again, 'When You Change Your Name, You Change Your life'

Your name is not who you are, it is who you look like, so people treat you like that and to some extent and purposes you behave like that.

Let me explain, my full name, 'Joanna Elizabeth Soley' vibrates at the energy of 3 - The Communicator. This is playing out under the level of consciousness, a vibration of how I appear to others. If you look at my branding, my website, see me on stage, hear me on a podcast, see me in all my leopard print wearing glory - this sums up the energy of how I am 'seen'. I appear to be very Life Path 3 - communicative, good company and a people person. However behind closed doors, I am not very 3 - I am very 1,4,8,9,22 - my full numeric chart, the 3 energy is how I am seen and appear to others, so people treat me like that, so to all extent and purposes I behave like that. Make sense?

Words are spells, that is why we call it spelling!

Letters are made up of numbers and numbers carry a numeric frequency. So, when you change your name you change these numbers, you then change how you are seen. I have never changed my name 'Joanna Elizabeth Soley' - has always been my name and has always vibrated at a 3 energy = The Communicator, so this is how I have always been seen in my life and business. However, if I changed my name this would potentially change how I am seen.

Have you changed your name? How did you feel when you did? Energetically people would have seen you through the lens of a different numeric energy with each name change.

Our names are incredibly powerful, showing us how we are seen in our businesses.

CHAPTER 37

HOW THE FIRST LETTER OF YOUR FIRST NAME IMPACTS YOUR BUSINESS SUCCESS

The first letter of our first name is the energy we first put out into the world ...

Names carry significance and the resonance of your name holds tremendous power. The first letter of your first name gives a strong indication of how you appear to be. This in turn can develop into how people treat you and then to some extent you will come to behave like this.

What does the first letter of your name mean for your business success?

Your first initial is the number that people FIRST see you as. It is not the whole picture of who you are, but it is your first foot forward into the business world.

The first letter of your first name is sometimes called the cornerstone in numerology and this is how you appear to people the first time they meet you.

The first letter of the first name in business is the very first thing we notice about someone.

We see this when ...

- Networking or introducing yourself (if you are wearing a badge or not).
- We see names in print.
- We look at websites or social media.

- We walk past someone at an event - this is the energy that will be picked up.

This is the energy we first put out into the world.

Below I connect you to the meaning behind the first letter of your first name ...

Using the alphabet, A = 1, B = 2 C = 3 etc. When we get to J = 10 - we reduce to 1 and start again, as J = the 10th letter of the alphabet = 10 = 1 + 0 = 1.

K and V are the 11th and 22nd letters of the alphabet so we do not reduce these as they are master numbers.

The letter of the first word dominates all the letters that follow it. If the letter of your first name vibrates as the same energy of your Life Path number, this intensifies that energy.

So, for example, my name Joanna = J = 10 = 1 = The Leader and I am a Life Path 1 = The Leader. What you see is what you get.

This can be a strong energy; I am definitely what it says on the tin with regards to all things 1 energy. This is the first 'flavour' people will pick up on when they meet you and then when they get to know you on a deeper level other numeric energies will kick in.

It is super-powerful to understand how we are first seen in business. Your name affects how other people react to you, on hearing a name people make unconscious assumptions about a person before they even meet. Your name gives you the vibrational energy you need on your business journey.

Get ready to appreciate how others see you in business!

So that you can ...

- Understand why they are treating you in a certain way!

- Consciously use this energy in your business and marketing strategy.
- Deliberately and intentionally work with this vibration instead of against it.

To put this into context – let me show you an insight into the energies ...

A J S all vibrate at = 1 ENERGY = INDEPENDENT

As the first energy of the first name, it encourages ...

A = Leadership
J = Good judgement
S = Ambition

A = As the 1st letter it encourages Leadership

Look at the shape of the 'A' - it thrusts itself into the world. The words associated with 'A' are Action, Ambition, Adventure etc. In business 'A' can be assertive and when it needs to be aggressive. 'A' is seen as The Leader, with original ideas and ambitious plans. There is an assurance about 'A', it is self-reliant. It prefers being busy to sitting still. It can be seen as direct and impatient.

J = As the 1st letter it encourages Good Judgement

'J' has leadership qualities. Look at its curved base, it can rock from side to side so not as secure as it seems and will sometimes need support. 'J' has a strong sense of self and prefers to be busy. If proceeds with caution it achieves its ambitions. 'J' takes an organised and systematic approach in business. It needs money to feel secure.

S = As the 1st letter it encourages Ambition

'S' can have wins and losses and experiences ups and downs in business and life, which can be seen in its shape. Success and self-esteem will be important. 'S' can, but sometimes prefers not to lead. Powerful and shrewd, 'S' has the ability to think strategically. It encourages ambition, although can become too self-involved.

B K T all vibrate at = 2 ENERGY = EMOTIONS

As the first energy of the first name, it encourages ...

B = Cooperation
K = Inspiration
T = Trust

B = As the 1st letter it encourages Cooperation

Can be introverted, look at the 2 parts of the letter 'B', they are enclosed, indicating the potential to be reserved. In business 'B' often works well in partnership or in a team as naturally cooperates with others. It can be sensitive, often preferring to follow rather than lead as can need outside motivation. 'B' can deal with details and is good at seeing all sides of a story.

K = As the 1st letter it encourages Inspiration

This is the 11th letter of the alphabet and a master number (see Chapter 6). K's have the ability to inspire others in business. They are here to help humanity on a large scale. It can cooperate with others, but it will not like being second best. 'K' can be intense so can create a nervous atmosphere around it. 'K' is able to be a high achiever but will have to safeguard against self-doubt and insecurity.

T = As the 1st letter it encourages Trust

Look at the shape of the 'T' - nearly a cross, so can have the tendency to be a bit of a martyr. Loving, loyal and makes friends easily in business. Not always comfortable in competitive situations, preferring to follow than lead. T does have the ability to teach. Can be highly strung as can sometimes feel nervous energy.

C L U = all vibrate at 3 ENERGY = OPTIMISTIC

As the first energy of the first name, it encourages ...

C = Creativity
L = Sociability
U = Fun

C = As the first letter it encourages Creativity

'C' can express itself well and is outgoing, look how 'C' is open on one side. A creative letter in business. It performs well before the public and will like attention. Can sometimes feel restless and easily thrown off balance. Can have money issues as it likes to spend.

L = As the 1st letter it encourages Sociability

'L' can experience sacrifices in life and business. It has a magnetic attraction - as it is an expressive letter that draws people towards it. 'L' prefers the lighter side of life. It is more settled and secure than it first appears and has the ability to plan in business. Can cope with complex situations but may be critical when opposed by others.

U = As the 1st letter it encourages Fun

Communicative and open but easily thrown off balance, look at the shape, open at the top with a bottom that can rock from side to side. 'U' thrives on contact with others. It attracts good fortune but can equally lose it. Can be in two minds at times. Needs consistency in life and does not like to be told what to do in business.

D M V = all vibrate at 4 ENERGY = ORGANISED

As the first energy of the first name, it encourages ...

D = Practicality
M = Hard work
V = Achievement

D = As the 1st letter it encourages Practicality

Brings patience and efficiency to life and business. 'D' is not scared of working hard for what it wants. Promoting orthodox thinking. Has the ability to create plans that work and gives personal security. Self-disciplined but sometimes overly cautious. Its shape is enclosed, so must avoid getting stuck in a rut.

M = As the 1st letter it encourages Hard work

Can experience ups and downs in life, which can be seen in the shape of the 'M'. Extremely practical and hardworking in business. Strong-willed, but will compromise rather than lose everything. Conservative with good ability to concentrate. Can be moody if change is enforced upon them.

V = As the 1st letter it encourages Achievement

This is the 22nd letter of the alphabet and a master number (see Chapter 6). One of the most powerful letters in the whole alphabet. It helps create change for others by developing dynamic plans that work. Highly perceptive and intuitive with strong psychic potential. Nervous tension can overpower it from time to time. It can be ruthless in business.

E N W = all vibrate at 5 ENERGY = CURIOUS

As the first energy of the first name, it encourages ...

E = Communication
N = Popularity
W = Versatility

E = As the 1st letter it encourages Communication

Provides a versatile and adaptable approach. 'E' offers the potential for great success in business. Look at the letter 'E', it is open at the side showing ability to communicate but its lines are straight, so is direct in its nature. Restless, with a love of change, it needs freedom. Copes well with setbacks in business, being flexible and adaptable.

N = As the 1st letter it encourages Popularity

Enjoys change in all aspects of life. Likes to be around others, occasionally over doing it on the social scene. 'N' helps attain public recognition in business. When self-disciplined it can achieve what it wants. It can tend to repeat mistakes and sometimes lacks confidence.

W = As the 1st letter it encourages Versatility

Look at its shape, like waves, 'W' can have a life of ups and downs. 'W' needs freedom in life and business, enjoying life to the full. Fun and variety are needed as much as work. A difficult letter to pin down. Well-meaning but can be disorganised.

F O X = all vibrate at 6 ENERGY = RESPONSIBLE

As the first energy of the first name, it encourages ...

F = Friendship
O = Study
X = Magnetism

F = As the 1st letter it encourages Friendship

'F' has the need to achieve harmony and balance in life. It is not as secure as it may appear and sometimes ignores the rules. Friendly and creative. In business 'F' often uses its voice successfully. It is capable of handling responsibility, but it needs creative fulfilment. Can experience self-doubt.

O = As the 1st letter it encourages Study

Representing the Magic Circle, 'O' is studious and retains what it gains. A good letter financially, as its will power and self-discipline are strong. 'O' is like the sun, look at its shape, it can be warm and attracts attention. Can have the tendency to bend the rules in business.

X = As the 1st letter it encourages Magnetism

A letter of high voltage - 'X' marks the spot! There are not many names where 'X' is the first letter. It helps with public recognition. It can symbolise sacrificing oneself to a cause or belief. Underneath its persona, it is exacting in its attention to detail. It requires a more settled lifestyle than it first appears. Can experience heavy burdens in business.

G P Y = all vibrate at 7 ENERGY = RESERVED

As the first energy of the first name, it encourages ...

G = Self-reliance
P = Self-knowledge
Y = Perception

G = As the 1st letter it encourages Self-reliance

'G' can choose whether to communicate or withdraw into itself and often prefers solitude. This mysterious letter has creative potential. It works hard for what it believes in business and can sometimes be private, even secretive. It can be obstinate.

P = As the 1st letter it encourages Self-knowledge

It has intellectual intensity and is drawn to deep thinking in many aspects of life. In business 'P' will probably be faced with astonishing events. It is strong minded and dislikes interference in its plans. It can work well with the right partner.

Y = As the 1st letter it encourages Perception

This letter will be faced with many choices in business - look at the way Y resembles a fork in the road. It will find it hard to commit to a single course of action. 'Y' helps intellectual work. 'Y' is beneficial in any business which involves research and development. Psychic or intuitive ability is enhanced with 'Y', but the flip side of this is the potential for indecision.

H Q Z = all vibrate at 8 ENERGY = DECISIVE

As the first energy of the first name, it encourages …

H = Financial Skill
Q = Business Acumen
Z = Power

H = As the 1st letter it encourages Financial Skill

'H' is a materially powerful letter. It will enjoy climbing the ladder of success - look at its shape. It sets goals and works towards what it wants with natural financial acumen. 'H' is independent. It is open to new situations and aware of its spiritual needs. H has a strong personality, which sometimes can be overwhelming for others in business.

Q = As the 1st letter it encourages Business Acumen

'Q' is eccentric and unusual. Financially astute, it has a distinctive way of operating in business, often using its intuition. 'Q' enhances physical skill. It can make mistakes in judgement, but a good letter for anyone in the business world.

Z = As the 1st letter it encourages Power

'Z' is often compared to a flash of forked lightning, look at its shape. Promotes recognition. There is an innate power and a love of luxury and status. An interest in metaphysics or spirituality can be present. A comfortable home life is important for 'Z'. A good letter financially. Z can be unconventional in business.

I R = all vibrate 9 ENERGY = CARING

As the first energy of the first name, it encourages ...

I = Idealism
R = Determination

I = As the 1st letter it encourages Idealism

Emotional and independent 'I' knows what it wants and dislikes interference from others. 'I' can be inspirational and entrepreneurial especially if the business has a humanitarian dimension. In business 'I' can have a dramatic and forceful personality.

R = As the 1st letter it encourages Determination

'R' needs to balance its humanitarian instincts with a need for action and achievement. In the past it was dubbed the 'growling' letter. It willingly assists others but may be taken advantage of at times. In business it is prone to over-giving and under-charging.

CHAPTER 38

YOUR BUSINESS IS ALIVE

A business is alive. It has its own Akashic records.

It has its own name, character, style, brand, colour, flavour and much more. Because it is alive it attracts and repels according to its nature (like we do) and its nature can be revealed through its numerology.

In a solo-entrepreneur situation, the numbers of the person running 'the show' are very important. Over time, as the business identity itself gains hold, the numbers of the business - its Life Path and its deeper numeric chart, will start to operate independently of the numbers of the business owner.

When the business grows with more online presence, a larger client base, a bigger team, employing contractors, moving to bigger premises (if applicable), the energy of the business will step to the fore. Ultimately this is where the business develops a life of its own and sustains itself almost regardless of what the business owner does.

G O O G L E

7 6 6 7 3 5 = 34 = 3 + 4 = 7

7 = The Seeker = the seeker of wisdom = Google = a search engine of information!

Prime Motivation

What is the prime motivation that your business is operating from? Understanding and harnessing this energy enables us to connect to the Life Path of our business.

Vibration

The word vibration in numerology is important. The theory of numerology rests on it. Everything in the Universe vibrates and by using numbers in the form of metaphysical arithmetic, we can apply these vibrations as numbers to our business and lives. What vibration is your business here to master?

Opportunities

When your business numeric energies are in alignment doors open. Cosmic tumblers align and opportunities are presented. Your business will attract opportunities that are a vibrational match with its numeric energies. What opportunities is your business here to attract?

It is important to understand the numeric energies of your business, by looking at the Life Path and the name of the business.

This in turn helps you to understand ...

- How your business name appears to your clients and community - the vibration they see.

- The Life Path number of your business and what it requires from you at the helm.

- The gifts that your business has and the impact it is here to bring to the world.

Appreciating your Business energies is a deeper piece of work that I do 121 with my clients -
https://josoley.com/bizology-sessions/

PART 7

DIGITS & DESTINY

CHAPTER 39

YOUR PRICING

Your pricing carries a numeric frequency, as your pricing is made up of numbers – e.g., £11, £22, £99, £197, £1997, £111, £1111, £2222 etc.

These prices carry a numeric energy. It is important that we understand what this is as this is the numeric energy that your products and services are being sold at.

When considering your pricing we also need to consider your personal numeric energies PLUS The numeric energies that your products and services carry.

Repetitive numbers are now popular with pricing, £11, £111, £1111, £22, £222, £2222, however business owners are using these numbers without understanding what they mean AND if these numbers are actually in alignment with their numeric energies and the numeric energies of their products and services.

When appreciating the numeric energies of your pricing it is important to consider ...

1. Your own numeric energies - what are you here to do in business?

You may be working with ...

Creative energies – 3s, 6s and 9s.

Communicative energies - 3s and 6s.

Dynamic energies – 1s, 5s and 8s.

Determined energies - 4s and 8s.

Spiritual energies – 2s, 7s 11s, ... Etc ...

2. What are the target energies that you want to bring into your business?

Are your products and services ...

Strategic?

Technical?

Creative?

Spiritual?

3. The cumulative energies of the pricing

Add up the complete price. It is not the individual energies so £1111 = 4. If you choose to use 4 in your pricing, are your products and services related to the energy of 4, are you, as the business owner working with the energy of 4?

4. Being mindful when using 8

Yes, 8 is about success and wealth but is this the energy of your business, products and services and are you working with 8 energy in your chart?

8 = The CEO / The Boss

8 is about success and wealth, abundance and money.

In business terms 8 is about ... Accomplishment, Ambition, Discipline, Goal Setting, Leadership, Organisation and Professionalism.

8 is THE Business number.

Business owners try to make their business fit to the number 8, and use it across their pricing, dates of events, products and services. This will not necessarily work if you or your business are not working with the energy of the number 8. Your numbers will carry a target energy, your business will carry a target energy, so it is important that you understand your numbers and what they mean in relation to what you are here to do in business.

5. Be mindful on when you use 11s and 22s e.g., £11 / £1111 / £22 / £2222

If you are going to use repetitive numbers when pricing, ensure that you understand master number energies and their cumulative energy (11 = 11 / 1111 = 4 / 22 = 22 / 2222 = 8). It looks good and it is on trend, but master numbers are HUGE (see Chapter 6), so make sure that you understand the vibration of these before you use them.

It is important that you understand your full numeric business picture before you create your prices.

In The Bizology® Pricing Strategy Session we look at ...

- Your numeric energies and what these mean for your pricing strategy.
- The numeric energies of your products and services and what these mean.
- The energies of your pricing, giving you hints and tips to help you align your pricing, so it works for you.
- What the cumulative energies of your pricing represent.
- What the number 8 means ... when and when not to use it.
- Appreciating when using master numbers 11s, 22s. 33s - e.g., £11 / £1111 / £22 / £2222 / £33 / £3333 – what impact this has on your pricing.
- The VAT Question when it comes to using numerology in pricing.
- 4 special cases that we need to be aware of.

And so much more ...

So that you can ...

- Understand your energies in alignment with your pricing.

- Understand the target energies of the products and services that you want to bring into your business with regards to pricing.

- Ensure your pricing is optimising your selling potential!

You can book your Bizology® Pricing session here ...
https://josoley.com/revolution-packages/

CHAPTER 40

UNDERSTANDING WHAT THE ENERGY OF YOUR HOUSE NUMBER / NAME MEANS FOR YOUR BUSINESS SUCCESS

Houses hold energy. Your house number reflects this energy.

When I was buying a house, its number was very important. I am a Life Path 1, so living in a number 1 house would have been perfect for me, innovative and independent in energy.

Also, an 8 house would have worked, as that is a key numeric energy in my chart – professional, high standards and goal setting.

I avoided a 4 house as I have a lot of 4 in my chart being born on the 4th of the 4th, 4 can be fixed as it's about foundations and work. Living in this energy would have felt heavy for me. There were other numbers I avoided as they would not have worked with my numeric energies. I nearly bought a 7 house and that would have been a place of solitude.

I bought a 6 house. 42 =4+2=6. It is also plot 177 =1+7=7=15= 6.

6 is about relationships, responsibility, love and connection. For my business living in a 6 house means working deeply with my clients and understanding what they need. In my personal life, living in a 6 home relates to family, friendships and neighbours, people will visit and it will have a loving, nurturing energy.

Many business owners work from home. Since the pandemic more people than ever are working from home. So more than ever it is important to understand how the number of your house supports you in your business, as this is the energy of the property you are working under.

The number of your home or place of work is related to the energy of how you operate and show up in business

Below I connect you to the energies of your house number and explain what this means to your business and life success.

Take your house number and reduce it to a single digit ...

For example, if you live in a ...

12 house = this is reduced to 1+2=3

44 house = this is reduced to 4+4=8

101 house = an 11 house (11 is a master number we do not reduce, we gently move the 0 out of the way).

202 house = a 22 house (22 is a master number we do not reduce, we gently move 0 out of the way).

11 house / 22 house = leave as these are master numbers.

If the house number has a letter after it like – 23A, A=1 as it is the first letter of the alphabet – so we would add 2+3+1=6.

If you have office premises across 2 units, for example - Unit 50 and Unit 51 = this gives you both a 5+0=5 and a 5+1=6 energy. Each unit will vibrate from a different energy and give you a different vibration to work from.

If your property has a name not a number, we work out the energy of the name, for example for Rose Cottage;

ROSE
9 6 1 5 = 21=3

COTTAGE
3 6 2 2 1 7 5 = 26=8

3+8=11 = The Spiritual Teacher

If you live in an apartment and it has a number and the building of the apartment also has a number, then both energies will play out.

Let's look at what the energy of your home means for your business success ..

If you live in a ...

House Number - 1 / 10 / 19 / 28 / 37 / 46 / 55 / 64 / 73 / 82 etc ...
The Leader House

- This will be an individual and independent home. You will need to spend some time on your own in this home.
- A great home to work for yourself and be self-employed, encouraging originality in your projects.
- A great place to start afresh in business, to create new beginnings.
- A unique, innovative and dynamic home for your business endeavours.
- Watch being too competitive or overambitious in this home.

House Number - 2 / 20 / 200 / 2000 etc ...
The Sensitive House

- This is a connection home, where harmony and balance are important.
- Encourages healing, good for a home-based therapy business.
- Business partnerships will flourish here with the willingness to cooperate.
- The interior decor and environment you work in will be important.
- Watch being too fearful or super sensitive in this home.

House Number - 3 / 12 / 21 / 30 / 39 / 48 / 57 / 66 / 75 / 84 / 93 / 300 etc ...
The Communicator House

- A great home to share your business message through all the platforms.

- It will attract people and be a social and networking home.

- Creativity and imagination will feature prominently, a good home for a home art studio.

- An optimistic and even a lucky home - watch your business expenses!

- Watch gossiping or being too critical of others in this home.

House Number - 4 / 13 / 31 / 40 / 49 / 58 / 67 / 76 / 85 / 94 / 400 etc ...
The Builder House

- A home to get your ducks in a row and create order and structure in your business.

- This home will want you to create a safe and secure business.

- Expect to work hard and focus on building foundations in your business.

- It will have a serious energy, helping you commit to your endeavours.

- Make sure you create the space to have some 'me time' in t his home.

House Number - 5 / 14 / 23 / 32 / 41 / 50 / 59 / 68 / 77 / 86 / 95 / 500 etc ...
The Adventurer House

- You won't be here long as a 5 home is about change!

- We can even go so far to say that you will travel away from this home or even rent it out.

- A 5 home will facilitate growth and expansion in your business.

- A home where you can elevate your personal brand in your business as Life Path 5s are popular.

- Watch out for too much indulging and temptation in this home.

House Number - 6 / 15 / 24 / 33 / 42 / 51 / 60 / 69 / 78 / 87 / 96 / 600 etc ...
The Nurturer House

- THE best home to run a family business. Relationships and responsibility will be the focal point.

- 6 is also very creative so this home can often be beautifully decorated.

- The perfect home for animals and home schooling.

- A good home to create, build and grow your business audience and community.

- Make sure you do not bite off more than you can chew in business in this home.

House Number - 7 / 16 / 25 / 34 / 43 / 52 / 61 / 70 / 79 / 88 / 97 / 700 etc ...
The Seeker House

- This home will call you to be a specialist in business and support any research and development.

- You will seek space and time off stage from the online world.

- Create a comprehensive library – as this is a good learning home.

- A 7 home is not really a social home, it is a sanctuary for contemplation.

- Be mindful of not being reclusive in this home.

House Number - 8 / 17 / 26 / 35 / 44 / 53 / 62 / 71 / 80 / 89 / 98 / 800 etc ...
The CEO House

- A great place for an investment as 8 is THE property number.
- You will feel a sense of authority in this home.
- It will be good for business as it will have executive energy.
- Ultimately a success and wealth home IF you apply yourself.
- Business has the potential to thrive here, the perfect home to create strategies, goals and plans AND to see them through.

House Number - 9 / 18 / 27 / 36 / 45 / 54 / 63 / 72 / 81 / 90 / 99 / 900 etc ...
The Humanitarian House

9 is about helping people so this will be ...

- A warm compassionate home where all feel welcome.
- A home to help people in business with their bigger vision.
- A good home to start a charity or foundation that is part of your business.

And 9 is also about endings...

- Completion of projects, finalising a part of your business and life.
- Watch your boundaries when you live in this home.

House Number - 11 / 29 / 38 / 47 / 56 / 65 / 74 / 83 / 92 / 101 / 1001 ...
The Spiritual Teacher House

- 11 is a master number, so this home will have a 'special' feel to it.
- A great home for both personal and Spiritual growth.
- A home to be inspired and inspire others.

- A home which will encourage you to develop your connection to Spirit.

- As 11 can be intense make sure that you have a direction and plan for your business under this roof.

House Number - 22 / 202 / 2002 / 2200 ...
The Architect of Change House

- A home with strong transformational energy as 22 is a master number.

- This 22 home will help you reach great heights and accomplish a great deal in business.

- Developing your spiritual connection will deepen your business connection.

- Will also require an element of 4 = structure, control, routine and system as 2+2=4

- Watch self-sabotaging in this home - destroying what you have created.

What number is your house supporting you to do in business?

Houses have a heart centre and hold energy.

Knowing the number of your home / your place of work and what it is supporting you to create in business is revealing, as this energy holds a resonance for your business and what it helps you achieve whilst working here.

There are no mistakes you will get the house number you need at this time for your business

***The house number you live in will have a deeper meaning dependent on your own personal numeric business chart.

CHAPTER 41

HOW DO YOU COMMUNICATE?

What is your 'phone number showing you about your communication style?

Your 'phone number can reflect the energy you are communicating with. When I do this with my clients, their communication number often matches their Life Path number.

Take your phone number to work out your communication number ...

Mine is ..

07718123229

Add the digits up together ...

$0+7+7+1+8+1+2+3+2+2+9 = 42 = 6$

Do not reduce 11s or 22s as these are master numbers.

Here's an overview of what your communication number means:

1 - The Leader

With this number your communication style will be fast paced and dynamic. An independent and purposeful energy.

Hang up on ego and selfishness.

2 - The Sensitive

With this number your communication style will be linked to emotional connection and togetherness. A listening and cooperative energy.

Hang up on being super sensitive.

3 - The Communicator

With this number your communication style will be busy with texts and calls. An enthusiastic energy.

Hang up on gossip and being critical of others.

4 - The Builder

With this number your communication style will be about having plans and structure. An organised energy.

Hang up on being too cautious.

5 - The Adventurer

With this number your communication style will be based around opportunities and travel. A popular energy.

Hang up your impatience and haste.

6 - The Nurturer

With this number your communication style will be based around relationships and helping people. A loving energy.

Hang up on over-giving to others.

7 - The Seeker

With this number your communication style will be based around learning and obtaining information. A quieter energy.

Hang up on being too private.

8 - The CEO

With this number your communication style will be based around business endeavours. A strategic energy.

Hang up on straining after success.

9 - The Humanitarian

With this number your communication style will be based around compassion and helping others. A healing number.

Hang up on being over emotional.

11 - The Spiritual Teacher

With this number your communication style will be based around inspiring others and a spiritual connection. An illuminating number.

Hang up on overreacting.

22 - The Architect of Change

With this number your communication style will be based around change and action. A transformational number.

Hang up on operating from ego.

PART 8

TO INFINITY AND BEYOND

CHAPTER 42

WHY KNOWING YOUR NUMBERS IS NOT A 'ONE AND DONE'

Before I started Bizology®, I ran a business 'Your Brilliant Business Angel', and I wrote a blog entitled – 'Why Once Is Killing Your Heart Centred Business.'

It was written based on the premise that marketing works when it is consistent and persistent. Getting your message in front of your ideal client on a regular basis, showing them that you are qualified to solve their problems. Marketing does not work once, once is not enough.

Over the years I have worked with hundreds of business owners helping them get clarity in their marketing to create the results they desire. Imagine this scenario; I am with a client, drinking coffee in a posh hotel, they are excited to have a second pair of eyes on their business to get some fresh input and ideas. We discuss their current marketing activity, the activity they have actioned to date and their options going forward. When we go through each option, they then say to me 'I tried it once, but it didn't work.'

I'm thinking, 'You tried it once?' 'You wrote a blog once?' 'You created a Facebook Ad once?' 'You sent a press release to a publication which is perfect for your ideal clients once?' 'You tweeted once?' 'You sent an email to your invaluable list once?' 'You spoke at an event once?' 'You carried out a direct reach out campaign once?' 'You attended a network group once?'

You get the idea. I am not exaggerating, let's put this into context, take your house, maintaining a house takes work, that's why it's called housework. We need to change the beds, clean the bathroom, hoover the carpets, shop for food, clean the windows, mow the lawn, you get the picture - in order to maintain the house.

Can you imagine if these tasks were done once? The sheets would be walking off the bed, the bathroom would be a health hazard, nobody in your family would eat ever again and you would die.

Bear with me here ... business owners say to me, "I **know** I am Life Path 8 or Life Path 3 or Life Path 2" – as if that's it. Or "You told me my numbers" - I helped them work out their Life Path number, this is literally only the beginning, the tip of the iceberg. They may even say, "I don't need to do your sessions now as I know I am a Life Path 7 or Life Path 11 or Life Path 5".

It's not a case of knowing your numbers then that's it. Knowing your numbers is not a 'One and Done'. It's a lifetime's work.

Knowing your Life Path number, the day of the month that you are born on, the deeper numbers within your chart, the energies related to your name, your Personal Year and your personal cosmic currents, is literally only the very beginning.

The real work starts after the information is given to you

Years later after launching Bizology®, I am learning daily about my numeric energies and how they interact with each other.

When we start to understand our numbers in full polarity, the negatives, the positives, the strengths and the weaknesses, this is where the journey begins, and the real results take shape. Where the magic happens.

To experience even the smallest amount of numeric magic available to you, you need to live and work through your numbers, intuiting what they are here to teach you. Your numbers walk with you.

Yes, the rewards are great, however the 'work' needs to be done. By 'work' I mean that understanding our numbers is a muscle we need to exercise. 'Knowing' is not enough. The results come through understanding the subtlety of the numbers and how this plays out in our life, then appreciating what action needs to be taken to course correct our life and business.

This is serious stuff. I get the fact that you don't want to be put into a box (especially if you are a Life Path 5), it's not about labelling, it's about understanding the energies of the numbers we have been given to move forward in our lives to do the job we are here to do.

Numerology helps us by ...

- Giving us another way of doing things by providing a clearer path in which to head.

- Guiding us by helping understand ourselves on a deeper level, bringing Aha moments related to what is going on in our business and opening doors to possibilities.

- Showing us not only personality analysis but how we can make better decisions, providing spiritual empowerment, aligning our vision for our business with our personality.

Because ...

- The more we work on our numbers the more we connect to what we desire in our life and business.

- Bizology® is about tailoring your approach to your unique needs, so that you can be on-point, work with your vibration and attune to cosmic currents.

- From this place the right paths are taken, the right doors open, and the right opportunities will be shown to you.

That is why Biology® is not a 'one and done' – it's a 360 degree spiritual, personal and business journey.

When I deliver Bizology® sessions to my clients, I literally see light bulb moments on their faces when I show them how all their numbers fit together like pieces of a puzzle. A client once said to me 'Bizology® cuts through years of therapy', not to sound blaze but to share the incredible power of numerology and when used in business Bizology®.

Bizology® is cosmic guidance, remembering...

- If you are struggling or feel lost, you always come back to your Life Path and the day of the month you are born on.

- There are numbers that are easier to be and hang out in, so we need to be mindful of these.

- If we have an excess of a number it can reveal an extreme talent in an area, however it can also be very challenging.

- Some Personal Years can be testing years, there are years where we are being called to slow down.

- There are also upheaval and change years – however we need these years to reset.

- If you have a number, you have it for a reason.

- If you do not have a number - you do not have it for a reason

I have a lot of 1 energy in my chart - innovation, originality, dynamism and independence.

However, I do not have any 6 in my chart. Well I have 2xO's (O=15th letter =6 energy), 1 in Jo and 1 in Soley, and I live at a

42=6 house, but that is it. 6 is about relationships, responsibility and family. At the time of writing, I am 50, never married and no kids - this is the result of no 6!

I can have a loving relationship, but I don't NEED one, and this is what Life Path 1 with no 6 energy is all about. Lead not need. This translates into my business too - leading a group not being in lots of groups. Your numbers don't lie!

Bizology® - 'Using the Powers of Numerology to Elevate Your Business Success', is an individual journey, we are only ready and available for what we are ready and available for right now.

A journey of exploration where each insight we gain from the numbers helps us develop and expand our own awareness and knowledge of ourselves.

When you work in the positives of your number, life will not be perfect (as it is not meant to be) but you will experience a sense of rightness with your life.

From this place tiny tweaks and adjustments with your behaviour and awareness results in massive changes in your life and business.

Bizology® is not a one and done, it is a lifetime's work and always another level is available to us.

CHAPTER 43

YOU HAVE STARTED YOUR BIZOLOGY®
JOURNEY - NOW WHAT?

Through reading this book - 'Bizology® 101' would have ...

- Connected you some way to your Life Path number and showed you the best ways to 'activate' this number by capitalising on its superpowers and being conscious of the ways it can trip you up. See Part 2 - Your Life Path number in Business.

- Helped you understand top line how you navigate your Life Path number using your Approach number - the day of the month you were born on. See Part 4 - Your Bizology® Compass.

- Showed you how to work out the Personal Year that you are currently working in and gave you the foundations of what this means for your business. See Part 3 - Using Cosmic Currents in Business.

- Explained how people see you when they first meet you by providing some insights on what your first name means for your business. See Part 6 - Words are Spells that's why we call it spelling!

You now know some of the abstract information. Now you need to do the work. This involves a deeper level of self-enquiry, revisiting the above information, living out your Bizology®, testing and tweaking, literally pulling the trigger on your numbers.

When you know your ...

1. Life Path number.

2. Deeper numeric chart - Bizology® connects you to 4 other numbers.

3. Personal Year and deeper personal cosmic currents.

4. Energy of your name and related details.

5. Energy of your business and related details.

You can make thousands of connections to make the right choices in your life.

Working with me 121 is very powerful

I was born on the 4th of the 4th and as you know by now 4 is about structure, routine and system. I am a self-confessed workaholic and control freak. This is very 4 and means that I am super organised, don't forget anything and help you apply Bizology® meeting you where you currently are in your life and business.

When you embark on your Bizology® journey, everything is clearly presented so you can easily read and digest. A Bizology® Portal is provided for you so that you can review all your reports and recordings. My 4/4 helps you to access and apply the information on a deeper level.

The current trend is to sell group programs as you can sell more, lots of coaches and mentors say they get burnt out selling 121 as it involves a lot from them. I am a Life Path 1, so my energies work well 121. Yes, I do have a membership, The Bizology® Magic Circle where I continue to connect my members to their numeric energies in a group setting. However, before we get to this point I show you your numbers 121 as your numbers are unique to you.

There are 7.9 billion (ish) people in the world and there are 11 Life Path numbers – but this is just the beginning, there are many more energies I show you about your chart as ...

You + Numerology = Business Success.

You may have thought because you have read this book that you don't need to work with me …

This is just the beginning.

"The more you learn - the better life gets" - Arthur Norris

WHERE TO FIND ME

My website has lots of impactful and business changing content for you with various FREE resources for you to use to understand your numeric energies on a deeper level, guiding you through your Bizology® journey, so no numeric stone is unturned, no time is wasted and there is no doubt that you are in the right place ... www.josoley.com

My free Apps

Discover how to work out your Life Path correctly here - https://josoley.com/LIFE-PATH-APP/

Discover how to work out your Personal Year correctly here - https://josoley.com/personal-years-app/

Facebook

My Facebook business page is here ...

https://www.facebook.com/BizologywithJoSoley/

I have a free group - 'Your Brilliance in Numbers' - where the members can ask me questions about using their numeric energies in business ...

https://www.facebook.com/groups/1822294504674775

Instagram

You can find me on the gram here - @josoleybizology

LinkedIn

You can find me here - https://www.linkedin.com/in/jo-soley-50363423b/

I look forward to connecting.

BIZOLOGY® 101 MASTERCLASS

Read the book? Now watch the Bizology® Masterclass

I have created a free masterclass for you here

YOU + NUMEROLOGY = BUSINESS SUCCESS

A free masterclass guiding business owners who understand there is a force higher than they are – and how to harness it!

One size does not fit all, so the way that one Life Path number operates in business is very different from the next.

Bizology® is about placing you as a business owner at the centre of all your business efforts to increase impact and connection with your audience.

Your numbers show you how you can show up, stand up, shine and sell in your business.

So that you can ...

Connect and align with your numeric energies and their power to ...

- Manage changes more smoothly and with greater ease to create more flow in your business.
- Understand you are more able to control your destiny than you think you are and from this place you can achieve your goals.
- Create a plan to move forward on your divine business path with ease, from a flow of quantum movement.

In this numerology training, I will show you how to move forward by understanding the heart of you.

The more we work on our numbers, the more we connect to what we desire in our lives and business.

Helping you understand who you are at a deeper level and from this place business success follows as the approach that you take is authentic to you and ultimately you make a more significant impact in the world.

Watch the Bizology® - You + Numerology Masterclass here ... https://josoley.com/business-success-masterclass/

BIZOLOGY® SPEAKING

I am often asked to speak from the stage about 'Using Numerology to Elevate Your Business Success'. Why? Because it is so fascinating AND it genuinely leaves your audience with huge Aha moments! To book me to speak at your event, membership or mastermind email – jo@josoley.com / https://josoley.com/bizology-speaking/

NEXT STEPS

If you are interested in working with me through my Bizology® Sessions and Packages, you can book here - https://josoley.com/work-with-me/ If you would like to speak to me about your Bizology® experience book a call on the link below ... https://calendly.com/Bizologywithjosoley/20min?month=2021-04 or head to www.josoley.com to book a call.

CHAPTER 44

BIZOLOGY® IN ACTION

I am a Life Path number...

The Title = ...

My takeaways about being this Life Path number are ...

....

....

....

....

....

I was born on the .... of the month.

Which means that my Approach number is ....

My takeaways about my Approach number are ....

....

....

I am currently in a Personal Year ....

The main energies playing out in my business this year are ...

....

....

....

Until my birthday on the ....

and then I go into a Personal Year..

The main energies playing out in my business this year are ...

....

....

....

....

....

The first letter of my first name is...

I am seen in business as ....

I live at house number / name..

The energy of this house will support me by ....

....

....

....

GLOSSARY

Approach number

How you approach your Life Path number - the day of the month you are born on. It is easier to stay working in this energy, the trick is to master our Life Path number.

Bizology®

My blend of business coaching and numerology, showing you how you relate to the business world. You + Numerology = Business Success.

Cosmic Currents

The cycles and energies that are currently helping you navigate your life and business.

First letter of first name

Sometimes called the cornerstone, this is how you are first seen in your business by others.

Life Path number

The main number we use in numerology and Bizology® - showcasing the path you are here to take this lifetime, also called your 'Destiny number' - what you are destined to do in your life and business.

Master numbers

11,22,33 etc ... Unique and powerful numbers that have a bigger job to do in business, they are like other numbers on steroids.

Numerology

The study of the mystical relationship between numbers, letters and patterns. An ancient tool used to gain deeper knowledge of self, others and how we relate to the world.

Personal Years

We work in 9-year cycles and there are better years and easier years to do things. Your Personal Year shows you what is going on right NOW in your life and business.

Universal Years

We are all working under our individual Personal Years, Universal years show us globally what energy we are working under as a collective.

ACKNOWLEDGEMENTS

It is impossible to mention everyone who has helped me get to this point in my life and business - you know who you are. Below I have mentioned a few key people who have been integral to the birth of Bizology® and this book.

MY BIZOLOGY® 101 TEAM

Business Mentor Emma Holmes of Rebels and Rockstars, the real deal, a Life Path 1 - The Leader, who has helped me birth this book into the world. Being born on the 5th of the 5th - she uses the energy of expansion and growth to help me move forward. Emma has been there for me through thick and thin and gets me in every sense of the word.

Claire Smith I have worked with Claire for the last 7 years, she is my website designer, a whizz at copy and has helped many of my clients design their websites and create their branding. A true Life Path 6 - The Nurturer, she is unconditionally loving and kind and helped me edit this book, keeping my essence, thinking things through with her 7 seeking approach.

Tracey Tester For the gorgeous cover, a clever innovative designer, Life Path 1 - The Leader, who is super creative with a 3 approach. Thank you for holding space, your patience and understanding during this process.

Amanda Clarke My photographer, a Life Path 6 - The Nurturer, who takes the best photos of me, always understanding exactly what is needed. She has a 9 approach, rolls with the punches and is great at looking at the bigger picture.

MY BIZOLOGY® COMMUNITY

Since I launched Bizology® I have made some real friends (not just using the word friend for the sake of it) other business owners that I respect in the online community that have helped me grow my audience through showcasing me to theirs, as they truly believe in Bizology®.

Janet Murray Thank you for supporting me through your podcast, Christmas market, Courageous Content Live event, etc by generously sharing me with your loyal audience. A Life Path 6 - The Nurturer with a 3 approach, Janet is invested in groups and communities with the innate gift of communication.

Catherine Morgan For always cheerleading me through your platform and inviting me to Jersey to share Bizology® at your Wealthy Women Experience retreats. A Life Path 22 - The Architect of Change with a 9 approach, Catherine is here to change the world one woman at a time through her mission "To equip and prepare 1 million women to be financially resilient" and she is absolutely doing this with love and compassion.

Carole Bozkurt For generously inviting me to speak at your events be it 'Rich, Hot and Spiritual', 'Successful Selling on Social Media', 'Limitless Clients' etc, always supporting me - a Life Path 9 - The Humanitarian, I appreciate your professional edge = 8 approach.

Ali Meehan and Jackie Groundsell - For making me an international speaker when I spoke in Spain for the 'Make It Happen Conference', thank you for your continued love and support.

Julie Anne Hart My soul sister in life and business. Thank you for using your Life Path 2 - intuiton, collaboration and connection to support and share me with your tribes and community in the Peak District and further afield.

Laura Perkes For your no-nonsense Life Path 3 - The Communicator ability to say it how it is with your 5 approach. Laura and I like to keep it real by screenshotting when we see 11.12 instead of 11.11 - it's a thing! We are in those moments not as Spiritual AF as we like to think we are.

MY CLIENTS

For all the hundreds and hundreds of clients that I have taken through their Bizology® sessions, be it 1 session, a 5-session package, a VIP day, the Bizology® 3 month Immersion program, Bizology® Marketing Clarity Program etc. I appreciate every single one of you for opening your hearts to learn more about you through the lens of Bizology®. To be able to personally witness your growth has been an honour.

A SPECIAL SHOUT OUT TO ...

Marina Beech As Laura says you are my biggest cheerleader, Life Path 9 - The Humanitarian, we were destined to meet in Italy (I never book things on a whim like that!) and I value you being part of my inner circle. Keep sharing your Akashic magic through your seeking energy - 7 approach.

Anita Panayiotis I have loved watching your growth over the past few years, an incredible Medium, Psychic and Animal Communicator. Life Path 6 - The Nurturer, but always creating change, mixing things up and adding new things to your business tool kit with your 5 approach.

Margaret Trevillion For shouting about me from the rooftops - Life Path 22 - The Architect of Change. Well done for everything you have achieved in the Podiatry industry using your master number energy.

THE MEMBERS OF MY BIZOLOGY® MAGIC CIRCLE

My inner circle, my membership, The Bizology® Magic Circle, those of you who didn't want to stop at a session or program and wanted to continue to embed the game changing knowledge of your numbers into your life and business on a continued basis, I salute you all and thank you for showing up.

MY FAMILY

My Dad, Martin Soley, who as a Life Path 7 – The Seeker, diligently read every one of these 63,000 words! Thank you for going through everything with a fine tooth comb and not losing the real Jo Soley.

My whole family for maybe not really 'getting' what I do but believing in me and trusting that I have got this.

AND LAST BUT BY NO MEANS LEAST - YOU ...

Thank you for being curious enough to want to learn more about you through the power of Bizology®. Knowing your numbers really does increase your numbers!

ACCOLADES

Diving deeper into Bizology® brings profound results as these business owners share below.

"I worked with Jo to understand numerology in my business. I was absolutely blown away by Jo's knowledge and genuine interest in helping me with some challenges both personally and in business. She's become a trusted friend and I'd highly recommend her work to anyone wanting to explore the power of Bizology®. It blew my mind and has helped me to make decisions in my business."

Catherine Morgan

"I've known Jo for over 5+ years and worked with her both personally and professionally. I find Jo's work ridiculously intriguing and have found that her guidance through the art and science of Bizology® has really helped me to navigate my pathways as well as inspired a whole stack of creativity/ideas and inspiration. Professionally, Jo has worked with my community to deliver incredibly valuable content which I know has been hugely impactful to the way others view themselves and their direction. I recommend Jo as not only is she is an absolute leader in her field, but she is also kind, personable, compassionate, intuitive and a good human."

Emma Holmes

"Jo is a Business Strategist who really took the time to understand me using her arsenal of tools. She has amazing after-care, presentation of how I can perform at peak performance and depth of research into 'me'. Taking the time to send a personalised card left a long-lasting impression on me. Grateful for the business tools, thank you so much again."

Katrina Young

"Jo got me and my business on track and keeps me on track. I didn't know myself very well when I met Jo a few years ago, and I knew my business even less. With her knowledge of business and marketing, alongside the energetic power of numbers, I have taken action on Jo's advice and I and my business have grown from strength to strength. We laid a solid foundation for my brand, my website and professional image. Each time I dip in my business it breaks through to a new level. Highly recommend Jo as an inspiring speaker, coach and Business mentor."

Jessica Vassallo

"I started working with Jo to expand on my personal development journey. Having first encountered Numerology in 2018, I didn't feel called to explore further. Until a conversation with a friend about Jo and the light she sheds on your life! After six in-depth sessions, I have complete permission to be myself. Jo has taken the doubt out of decisions that I previously would have questioned and highlighted that my gut and intuition have a vital role when choosing the direction of my life. Jo has made sense of feelings and patterns in my life that I now realise are an integral part of who I am. If your life feels sticky or like it's not flowing, Jo will help you discover who you truly are and inspire you to be unapologetically you."

Alice Woodcock

ABOUT THE AUTHOR - JO SOLEY

The formal bit ...

Jo Soley, founder of Bizology®, is a Business Coach and Business Numerologist with over 25 years' experience in Business Development, Sales and Marketing. She uses the powers of numerology to help her clients elevate their business success.

Numerology is a well-established ancient science, which has been used by celebrities and CEOs across the world as a way of harnessing the subtle energies that create our unique blueprint.

The foundation of numerology is based upon the concept of uniqueness, it is a discipline that recognises every person and every situation as unique. This is its real power and value. One size does not fit all and there is no magic formula in business, Jo shows you how to align to your business purpose.

Bizology® grants access to higher-level business solutions. Understanding and connecting to her numeric energies has been pivotal to Jo's and her client's business success. It has helped her to approach all that she does from a position of strength, and it has given her a fresh perspective on doing business in the 21st century.

The fun bit ...

Jo is a lover of all things leopard print - as Life Path 1 and Aries this fiery energy is present not only in her character but in her wardrobe!

Jo loves a good coffee - caffeination is the key to business success.

Jo loves a good bargain - you will often find her rummaging around charity and pre-loved shops in the search for leopard print.

Stormzy - her guilty pleasure, he is also a Life Path 1. Jo loves his ethos, the #merky brand and the way he shows up for his community and people.

Sushi - it must be good Sushi - not any old supermarket Sushi!

St Lucia - having spent her 50th birthday there it is her new happy place.

B1ZOLOGY®

with Jo Soley

Printed in Great Britain
by Amazon

24303781R00169